G000066328

This volume first published to complement
the Fonteyn Phenomenon Conference
hosted by

Royal Academy of Dancing
Incorporating The Benesh Institute

Margot
assoluta

Margot
Fonteyn's
shoes
actual
size

Keith Money

ffi

*for Phoebe
and Lavinia*

Peggy and Felix, Christmas 1919

Published by Fair Prospect Imprint
PO Box 100-242, NSMC, Auckland 1330, New Zealand

First Published 2000

Copyright © Keith Money throughout

All rights reserved.
Without limiting the rights under copyright
reserved above, no part of this publication may be
reproduced, stored in or introduced into a retrieval system,
or transmitted, in any form or by any means (electronic, mechanical,
photocopying, recording or otherwise) without prior
written permission of both the copyright owner
and the above publisher of this book.
The moral right of the author
has been asserted.

Book designed by Keith Money

Set in Electra
Origination by Fair Prospect Imprint
Printed in China

A CIP catalog for this book is available from
the British Library, and the Library of Congress

Money, Keith
Margot assoluta.
1. Fonteyn, Margot, 1919-1991

Author's Note

The material of this book fell into the coils of the publishing world, soon after Margot's death in 1991; and that world, involved in its own turmoils, broke its promises to produce, correctly, the product which had attracted it in the first place. Expediency! The result was that it languished in store, in both the Northern and Southern hemispheres, for eight years. I have revived it now (and done most of the mechanical labours myself) prompted by a three-day symposium, The Fonteyn Phenomenon, held in London in September 1999, to celebrate the far-reaching accomplishments of a truly remarkable performer. Because it can be difficult for someone of one generation to relate to the life of someone belonging to a preceding generation – particularly in respect of the younger person's own variety of hopes and uncertainties – I have put in a section on the Fonteyn childhood, to show the apparently normal child who became the far from normal adult; although it will become clear that perhaps she was not so very normal, even when young. These pictures were given to me by Margot's father, who took most of them himself. In her autobiography, Margot painted a wonderfully clear-headed view of these beginnings, but it is in the very nature of such viewpoints to dodge around some of one's own strongest characteristics, and if there is a general lesson to be drawn from this particular child's life, then I believe it centres upon application, above all. This is a decision, for a young person; it is not some benediction which simply alights on the brow, unbidden.

Much of my text relies on anecdotes gleaned during my contact over a number of years with the dancer's entire family, so that what I describe here is exactly what the participants in the saga told me, first hand; and not only family; also prime mentors – and of course Margot herself. These 'footnotes' accrued over a decade, at a time when I had no conscious plan to save them as part of some master plan, so it has become like a palimpsest, with many layers of impressions, which is the way I have deliberately structured the book, rather than trying to disguise that. Some matters I have alighted on because Received Information is becoming layers of wrong on wrong; so, if I was privy to some of it, then, I may as well sort some of it, now. I would not pretend to understand the 'whys' of certain elements, even so; and as to the 'hows' of Margot's extraordinary capacities, there is always a mystery about such people. I think Margot was a mystery to herself, in a number of ways, and although her 'simplicity' of style and nature was widely remarked, it always seemed to me that she was an extremely complex – indeed, almost split – personality. It is doubtful if she could have survived some of the extremes of pressure which frequently descended upon her, had she been otherwise, and it surely requires a great complexity of resource to be able to suggest simplicity, without appearing merely simplistic; a rare art, in fact.

For this concluding volume of my personal quartet relating to Fonteyn, I went for images which still triggered a response in me, as the subject did thirty something years ago, but as a kind of challenge I chose only from images which previously I had not used. Margot might just have passed this, for the very reason of it; anyway, I shelter behind the excuse. My odyssey of photographing Fonteyn began with an image taken from a television screen in 1962, and the very last picture came from the same medium in 1986, when she made an introduction for a Royal Command Variety Performance – which also happened to celebrate the 50th anniversary of her first appearance on television. Undoubtedly, a phenomenon.

However theatrical stardom be measured – whether by box office queues, newspaper column inches, statistics of performance, or its degree of influence on a subsequent generation – it is almost impossible to quantify, or even understand fully, the sheer weight of attendant publicity, which makes a few names imperishable in one era and beyond. An ability to survive this remorseless daily pressure is one of the vital talents required of such a name. Of the two most renowned ballerinas of the 20th century, Anna Pavlova and Margot Fonteyn, it can be observed that both acquired their legend status as much by indomitable tenacity, as by any other of their extraordinary gifts, and that even when they had garnered worldwide fame, they guarded themselves against the soft options that such renown brings in it wake. In the unsparing world of

ballet itself, both women had the kind of courage which admits no retreat, with a quiet strength of purpose allied to an unshakeable interior conviction about the sheer act of dancing. They wanted it for its own sake, not for what it might bring; reward was as much in the business of class, as it was in public performance. Where Fonteyn's early career differed most markedly from the great Russian exemplar was in the matter of early goals; the young Pavlova's convictions had always been in some way intertwined with matters of her very survival, materially and artistically; for her, the element of competition could never be ignored. By contrast, the young Fonteyn for the most part was cushioned on a broad stream of other people's plans for her progress. She had the relative luxury of being groomed within a cosily domestic company on which no great expectation or weight of history rested, yet her progress was from the very start a matter of speculation and prediction. In the first month of 1931 Pavlova had died, a few days short of her fiftieth birthday. At the time, Fonteyn was an English schoolgirl in Shanghai, nursing a vague ambition towards chorus line or corps de ballet, in England. But within four years, at the age of fifteen, she was already marked out by London critics: "She should develop into a really great artiste." It was felt even then that she had the spark of something which could not be taught. Taking over a rôle in Frederick Ashton's *Les Rendezvous*, she was described in one newspaper as having "some of that intoxicating quality always associated with great dancers." Thus, the major requirement was careful nurturing, not manufacture.

If we look back on the 20th century in order to view the creation of British classical ballet in the 1920s, we can observe the paramount influence of Diaghilev's Ballets Russes; and also the example of Anna Pavlova's company, with its hints of steady employment and long seasons; and behind all that, the whole weight of the late 19th-century Russian tradition. Through the emerging English core are twined two arteries vital to the growth of the whole; one Polish, the other Anglo Irish. Cyvia Rambag was born in Warsaw in 1888 and Edris Stannus was born in County Wicklow in 1898; and of course the one became Marie Rambert and the other became Ninette de Valois. If the latter achieved her dream of a great national ballet company based in Lon-

don, she certainly could not have achieved it in the time, without the nucleus of talent which had been nurtured almost out of thin air by the senior of this apple-and-pear combination. To focus on the younger one, in this tale, is not to ignore the other in the scheme of things. What of ballet instruction in London in these formative years? The Russian-Italian influence was all-pervasive at the serious end of balletic endeavour in the capital; but academies of every hue bullied and cajoled children into being 'theatrical' – unless they were enrolled at Mrs Wordsworth's School, where Edris Stannus ended up after her family removed to England when she was eight. Mrs Wordsworth loathed the whole concept of professional dancing and did everything in her power to instill the same idea in her pupils. Ninette de Valois came to look back on the period between her tenth and fifteenth birthdays as "wasted years." But she was taken to see the leading dancers of the day, and inevitably became enthralled by Pavlova – so much so that she diligently made notes about *Le Cygne*, while watching from the upper circle. This effort proved useful once she had joined Lila Field's theatrical school, since a select group of pupils from that academy were herded around England for an annual tour, and expected to imitate various stage stars of the day. Inevitably, Edris was assigned La Pavlova, and began 'dying' each night, as the swan, for a salary of £4 per week – for which she was expected to make ten different solo appearances every night; all this at the age of fourteen. At least her inspiration had been the best; as she said of Pavlova, years later, "All my life I have remembered her intrinsic head movements, and that electrifying and magnetic flow."

During the 1914-1918 war, when Pavlova and her company were stranded in the Americas, dance employment everywhere was fractured, and Ninette de Valois (as she had become) took a job as the lead dancer in the pantomime seasons at the Lyceum; at least this was a forcing-house for general stagecraft. Then, at the war's end, the great Cecchetti started teaching in London, in the periods he was not required by Diaghilev, and de Valois was amongst a chosen few. This was a turning point in many ways. In 1921, when Diaghilev mounted for London his homage to Petipa, the exquisite, if ill-fated, Bakst production of *The Sleeping Princess*, the timing may have been wrong for audiences, but for the fate of Western classical ballet the moment was exactly right; its influence was to prove incalculable. De Valois loved everything about it, and she saw immediately that it contained the well-spring of a great tradition in its purest choreographic form. The challenge of performing such a work, correctly, could be the laboratory in which fresh talent (of whatever order) could only respond, and for the better. In the event, that 1921 production was eventually impounded by its creditors, causing Diaghilev to flee to the Continent with a much-reduced team. Still, de Valois set her sights on Diaghilev's power-base as being a vital fount, and she needed to get into the engine-house, to observe – just as Rambert had done,

a decade earlier. De Valois finally gained a position as soloist for the impresario, and thereafter she danced for his Ballet Russes company for three years, between 1923 and 1926 - at which point it could be observed that the company itself had lost any clarity of aim or purpose, beyond effect for effect's sake.

In 1927, Pavlova's company was exhaustingly involved in yet another of its English provincial tours, and on a Saturday night in November, they performed at the Bournemouth Winter Garden, on England's south coast. The following morning, while they were packing for their next stop in the marathon, thirty miles away in the direction of sunrise there was a ship about to depart for the United States, and amongst the passengers crowding the rails was eight-year-old Peggy Hookham from South London. Since our heroine appears, at this juncture, to be locked into a distinctly unpromising scenario: leaving behind everything that glittered in the world of theatre, we might seek here one further link in the chain which did eventually bring her to a place in the world of ballet. Casting a retrospective eye on distinctive juvenile dance talent in London at that period, we can note three stage-struck sisters in the Marks family and focus on the eldest, Lillian Alicia – a seemingly frail creature blessed with a constitution of steel. Quietly but determinedly she had persuaded her family to let her appear on the London stage in 1921, at the age of 10, show-cased in a pantomime item employing what was then known as Fancy Dancing. She was billed as Alicia Markova, and – inevitably – as The Miniature Pavlova. With that weight of expectation suddenly upon her, she left the Thorne Academy at Palmer's Green and began studying in earnest with Seraphine Astafieva in Chelsea; to such effect that by 1925, Diaghilev – no less – adjudged her sufficiently advanced at 14 that she could join his company. Under this exotic protection she was given, within a single year, not only soloist status but also two new solos, both created especially for her by a Russian expatriate, George Balanchine, who was a ripe old twenty-one. And all this in the heady surroundings of Monte Carlo! This seemingly ferocious exploitation of young talent did have its own publicity value – doubtless as Diaghilev intended, and it advanced a more general realisation (at least amongst those interested in dance as a paying profession) that children who missed an early start might expect to be swept aside, amidst a deafening patter from other smaller feet hurtling towards the footlights. Much of this theatrical precocity was written about quite learnedly, for subsequent fireside consideration, certainly the editor of the *Dancing Times* followed ballet and stage dancing diligently – along with the fare for his broader readership, which ran the gamut from ballroom to fan dancing. Copies of his respected journal ended up as far away as China, too.

In the constellation of good fairies attending the birth of British ballet, we must salute one more vital link in the chain: inimitable, indefatigable Miss Lillian Baylis, legendary manager (with, as she would always say, God's assistance) of the venerable Victoria Theatre, known universally as The Old Vic. She had inherited the running of this enterprise from her aunt, Emma Cons. The theatre stood in an insalubrious district on the south side of the Thames, but it provided a beacon of bargain-priced "quality" entertainment, and Baylis' commitment was unwaveringly "to provide the poor with the best". When this admirable policy produced more patrons than her building could squeeze in, she sought to pair it with another, eventually acquiring a broken-down site a mile and a half north of the river, in an equally shabby environ. This did indeed have a large potential audience, but even if it deserved the best, there was little sign that it could afford more than a slice of it. Baylis was undeterred. Ignoring awkward minor details – that she did not have the money was not insignificant – she set about the construction of a new building; and in 1931, at the height of the Depression, the Sadler's Wells Theatre opened for business, five years after Baylis had first listened sympathetically to Ninette de Valois' plans to establish a ballet company, with an attendant school. In the interim, Baylis had provided the de Valois dancers with sporadic employment within the framework of her opera and drama productions; now, she could offer them some sort of continuity with a seemingly permanent base. This haven in Rosebery Avenue had been achieved with faith, hope, and limited amounts of charity; plus, of course, God's assistance; in return, Miss Baylis hoped (and surely prayed) that she might eventually produce for her "dear people"

nothing less than the best. This ambition coincided with de Valois' aims, exactly.

Back to the ship leaving Southampton in November 1927: not unusually, the vessel was the instrument for a fair degree of emotional turbulence, and within the Hookham family up on deck, any upset centred on Felix Junior, firmly on shore. His age, eleven, had at this time placed him in that English middle-class wasteland which revolved around boarding school; because he was a boy, he could not be indulged in the frivolity of voyaging to China. Instead, custom demanded that he proceed through the rituals of becoming a complete Englishman, and much as he might have doubted the fact at this junc-ture, his apparent best interests were being placed by his parents well ahead of his sister's. Even if he had reached China, *en famille*, he would have passed a stream of Orient-based English boys all heading in the opposite direction – all of them plucked at a crucial moment from any risk of going irretrievably 'native'. It was felt that an English boy automatically surrendered his fullest identity if he was not under institutional lock and key by the time he reached puberty, and on that basis Felix stayed ashore in 1927. He was nominally in the care of his grandparents, but principally under the jurisdiction of Ripley School; his sister, by contrast, was heading off to what were assumed to be educational deserts in the outside world.

Kurdish style, in Gayaneh.

Cambodian style, in a presentation head-dress.

Rive Gauche, Paris, 1968
The students' rioting was
within earshot.

South China Seas, 1929
These love birds were
swept overboard,
during a severe storm.

15

As the only daughter of an English engineer (her English-born mother was part Irish, part Portuguese Brazilian) Peggy Hookham by the age of eight was travelling with her mother and father in America and the Far East, following the course of Mr. Hookham's postings with the British American Tobacco Company, most particularly in Shanghai. There, itinerant dancing teachers (of varying skill) all noted the child's receptivity to ideas of hard work and diligence. It was clear that a faintly exotic quality lay under the English reserve; the Portuguese genes manifested themselves in dark hair and eyes, and perhaps in a certain *gamin* element in the personality. There was no mistaking her physical aptitude: the body had perfect proportions which distributed stress evenly, and everything was harmonious to the eye. All remarked on her natural grace and the distinctiveness of those movements. Although the adult Fonteyn continually complained about soft muscles, which required extra work, she survived general wear and tear far better on the whole than dancers of more steely physicality; but when Ninette de Valois accepted the fourteen-year-old Hookham into the Vic-Wells Ballet in London, the child trailed a very mixed history of teaching. The feet, to the martinet de Valois' eye, were already in poor shape, and it took a strict regime and a change of ballet shoe to reverse this weakness. Throughout her career thereafter, Fonteyn lived with the feeling that her feet might sabotage her endeavours at any moment. The critics who predicted great things of the young girl saw, mainly, her simplicity

of effect; she forced nothing, and her insecurities (which were really quite marked) never disrupted performances. From the start, there was a gentle yet pervasive stage presence, of which the principal defining characteristic was a vulnerability that provoked feelings of protectiveness in audiences. The effects were certainly not large, yet there was an uncanny knack for avoiding any 'colour' that might appear out of key. The young Margot (she had contrived a variation of Margaret, and the Brazilian family name Fontes) displayed an intuitive sense of measure, and even when she found herself precipitated into the fierce light of centre stage, this equilibrium in great measure saved her from any damaging forms of excess, or self-regard.

Fonteyn's progression was almost remorselessly ordered. The early career was masterminded, of necessity, by de Valois, who knew that her company could not flower effectively unless it was led by a genuine and acknowledged ballerina, one who could lead by right and encourage by example. By a quirk of fortune, the fledgling British national company produced just that, exactly upon the hour, and almost immediately, the history of the company was inextricably bound with the advancement of this dancer, eventually passing the milestones of national approval and international acclaim in an apparently uninterrupted progression. Of course it was a company progress, and the particular talents at its head were distinctive on several counts, yet within all that, the basic requirement of theatredom: its burning

Paris, 1968
In the salon of the Plaza Athenée Hotel, with Margot reflecting on the fact that the same room held big vases of lilac on the occasion of her wedding reception.

hunger for 'stars', was safely assuaged by the early appearances of Fonteyn alongside the Wells' undoubted star, Robert Helpmann. The young Margot, slightly plump, charmingly unforced, was in no way swamped by Helpmann's suzerainty. Between the ages of sixteen and nineteen, Fonteyn was launched into the leading rôles of a series of major classical ballets – the like of which could not be seen anywhere else except Russia. If remnants of *Swan Lake* had been seen in the West, de Valois' ambition was always to reproduce a proper measure of the original, and with the help of émigré Russians, and with Constant Lambert, a musical director of uncommon skill, de Valois was able to underpin her aspirations with a solid measure of expertise, so that the learning curve rose from a secure base.

London theatre had undoubtedly benefited from the fact that Marie Rambert had already established in West London not only her own ballet school in 1920, but also a small performing group in 1926, which did pioneer work in fostering home-grown talent, both in dancing and choreography. When Alicia Markova's early career stalled upon the death of Diaghilev, and she returned to London, it was to dance in a production of Dryden's play *Marriage à la mode*, mounted for the Lyric Theatre. The choreography for this production came from a young Rambert protégé, Frederick Ashton. Markova's next rôle, for the Camargo Society, was choreographed by de Valois, who knew her from the Diaghilev company; so notions of shoe-string endeavour, always

associated with these London experiments in the early thirties, cannot disguise the fact that the raw talent itself was of extraordinary order, on several levels.

By 1935, the modest performing schedules at the Wells, twice a week at most, may have suited tyros, but they proved restrictive to Markova, who was by now in full flight as a performer. She felt the need to venture further afield, and her departure from Sadler's Wells was an alarming event for the young company. De Valois treated the matter as one more weekly challenge, and set about stitching the gap. Her hopes for mounting full-scale classics, particularly the big Petipa ballets, were always to adhere, as scrupulously as possible, to the source material; and once the framework had been achieved to her satisfaction, nothing was allowed to be altered thereafter. In deciding that the young and immature Fonteyn carried with her the possibilities of ballerinadom, de Valois was undertaking a huge act of faith, for although the girl was clearly special, physicalities alone made it difficult for her; she lacked any great elevation, and at that stage was really quite plump, and yet she was required first off to find the measure of the old Romantic ballet *Giselle*, which had been a cornerstone of the repertoire as long as Alicia Markova danced the lead. The loss of Markova was particularly frightening for a girl who had admired the senior dancer so unreservedly; all of her initial ideas about a ballerina stemmed from the Markova style. Despite certain limitations, from the start Fonteyn endeared herself to audiences in *Giselle*. If some of her performances were muted and small-scale at that time, it was because she would not stray beyond her interior conviction. She would listen diligently to advice and instruction, though it was often months (and in one instance, years) before she would alight on the real truth of it for herself, and thus fill the final corners of the portrayal.

After *Giselle*, in orderly succession she was put into *Swan Lake*, first the white acts only, and then the dual rôles of Odette and Odile. The fright of attempting these rôles was very marked for Margot. Her personal diffidence did not really allow her to build confidence, but she had the unqualified support of the team around her, and the theatrical craftiness of Helpmann as her partner. Such external security did allow her to develop at her own pace. Audiences, too, were tolerant. Though the productions of the big warhorse classics were painfully scant (judged by postwar standards) in England the company had no rival on the horizon. For a young Sadler's Wells ballerina, beyond the showcase rôles of pure and daunting classicism, there were numerous one-act ballets, almost bewildering in their variety. All these were sustained by the faithful local audience. These shorter works were welcome relief from the terrors of the big ballets, and provided a tyro with a wonderfully broad early platform. However, the teenage Fonteyn had a shaky start in her work with the company's principal choreographer, Frederick Ashton, who found her resistant and technically imprecise. A rapport was only established when he recognised the young girl's underlying seriousness of purpose, and her healthy measure of self-criticism. He then began to shape a sequence of ballets around her, giving her rôles which drew on varying shades of characterisation, from lightly brushed-in pathos and innocence, to rôles of hard-headed glamour which required precise comedic skills, as well as technical attack. Her deftness with comedy was subsequently seen to fine effect in *Coppélia*, and several of Ashton's cameos for Fonteyn drew on her willingness to risk self-mockery.

As a teenager, Fonteyn's basic personality was sunny and uncomplicated; in fact throughout her career introspection was markedly alien to the Fonteyn persona. This general level-headedness steered her safely past many of the usual adolescent danger points. Ashton was later to admit that Fonteyn's exceptional natural musicality, allied to markedly expressive arms, led him to explore areas of lyricism he might otherwise have bypassed, so that between them, choreographer and muse turned this particular quality into a natural expression. Having a ballerina who could draw the eye without fuss or contrivance meant that Ashton could, at key moments, risk emotion as an intrinsic element, always conveyed with the most delicate of nuances. These 'veils of colour', made potent by their very understatement, provided the real key to most of Ashton's Fonteyn rôles. In terms of structure, some of the weightier moments are off the page, choreographically speaking, with the meaning somehow embedded in certain transitional passages. Many of the rôles have the usual Ashton hallmarks of filigree detail; yet despite her feelings of technical inadequacy, Fonteyn would master the sequences by degrees until they re-emerged as a natural expression of mood summoned, so it seemed, without effort or even pre-thought. Ashton had been obsessed by Pavlova's stage personality and her electric effects, and younger English dancers were often intimidated by his extolling such vibrant stagecraft. But the young Fonteyn was slowly developing her own stage personality. Her theatrical power was pervasive, in the manner of a subtle perfume; the sharp, thunderbolt flash was not her forte. The key lay in the rare evenness of her talents, with no over-accentuated highlight. Where other dancers would contrive to arrive at a series of peaks in performance, Fonteyn's exposition of a rôle somehow unspooled with an unbroken dramatic tone, everything filtered through some internal prism which released all the colours evenly, so that the performance was always difficult to unstitch and analyse, subsequently. Undoubtedly, concentration lay at the heart of it. It produced a slightly baffling brand of star quality. So consistently did she hide all the joins – no matter what internal demons were at work – that nothing disrupted the seamless presentation. This evenness astounded contemporaries who had the opportunity to observe her on long foreign tours, performing under all manner of distraction or inconvenience. As a small itinerant

company in wartime, the Sadler's Wells Ballet had performed at times under almost crushing rigours, and it was then that Ninette de Valois wondered whether this exceptional (and malnourished) work load would wreck Fonteyn's long-term prospects.

The way the Sadler's Wells Ballet stormed New York for the first time, in 1949, has become one of the more frequently re-worked pieces of ballet lore. Inescapably, at the heart of it lies Fonteyn's mastery on the night; she was transfixed with nerves, yet managed to run on stage as if she had no care in the world, so totally in control of her vocabulary that the audience revelled in the message; indeed, at the end of the Rose Adagio she hit such a perfectly sustained balance that she could dismiss the third prince's proffered hand with a deliciously teasing turn of her head. History was made: "the world's only valid legend," said a newspaper the following day. She was on the cover of *Time* magazine, and suddenly world property. This was vital to the company's long-term prospects, because however worthy the contemporary English ballets may have been, the critical response to them was sniffy. It was acclaim for a great dancer (in a great Tchaikowsky/ Petipa ballet) which kept the queues forming, initially - and even *Swan Lake* had a struggle. Margot could always be reduced to helpless giggles by any reference to the review which stated that "four acts of swans is a lot of swans!" But, from that first trip to North America, the company itself won sufficient loyal supporters that there was talk of a return visit,

Accepting applause in Athens,
after Birthday Offering.

almost before the first tour was over. Fonteyn was now regularly partnered by Michael Somes, and this pairing led a four-month tour of America and Canada in 1950 – the first of many similar cavalcades which saw an increasing army of American fans coming under the spell of the big classical ballets. Fonteyn was firmly established as an international celebrity, but despite tempting offers from many quarters, she chose to remain within the company she felt was her 'home', accepting the less than spectacular salary that went with the job.

When Fonteyn could be persuaded to discuss her own career – a rare enough occurrence with one so determinedly against self-analysis – she averred that her life was quite unplanned, that she dealt with each day as it came along, and that the longevity of her theatrical career astonished her, as much as anyone who observed it. Behind the carefully guarded remarks of one who felt that, perhaps she *had* "learnt one or two things" during her days in ballet, there was a performing animal whose very life-blood was given meaning by performance. It is true that she could have been happy doing some other job (and doing it well) yet it has to be said that she was careful never to allow the circumstance to arise. She could accommodate a private life, but only in as much as that life somehow accommodated the other. It was a juggling act, at which she was very skilled.

By the time Fonteyn had passed her fortieth birthday, most onlookers were counting themselves fortunate in catching what might be "one of her last performances". This fever of autumnal melancholy did nothing to spoil the acclaim for each immaculate performance. There was no obvious reason for Fonteyn to quit the stage; the figure was trim and supple, a marked improvement on her teenage form. Her stagecraft was apparently inexhaustible. She had the gift of her unchanging oval face, with its huge dark eyes, either haunting or magnetic or sparkling with fun, which could be read from every corner of an auditorium. The general effect was glamorous, impeccable – and occasionally, slightly remote. Fonteyn herself still took each day as it came along. She dismissed any mention of retirement, and was casually amused at the energy spent by others in mapping this milestone.

In 1961, the arrival in the West of Rudolf Nureyev, at a time of considerable political tension with Russia, provided overnight a talking point that spread far beyond artistic enclaves. Ballet was suddenly general news. When the story finally became linked to Britain's prima ballerina, Covent Garden found itself besieged. The press corps, old hands at helping to embroider any story concerning Fonteyn, now scented unguessed new mileage, with the announcement that Fonteyn would dance with the young exile. Fiery young Tartar meets Queen of Ballet! Beyond the brouhaha, the actual theatrical frisson of this partnership was greater than any prediction. Like the best recipes, it lacked much calculation. Fonteyn, in organising one of her annual charity galas for the Royal Academy of Dancing (of which she was president – also elected against her will) was seeking likely drawcards for the latest programme, and had passed an invitation to the young renegade, then in Denmark taking classes with one of Fonteyn's former teachers, Volkova. Nureyev had never had any opportunity to see Fonteyn, but for him, "name was magic." Unabashed, he instantly asked to partner Fonteyn at the gala. She declined the request, (in her phrase, she thought it suggested "mutton dancing with lamb,") but was pleased that the young man would appear with others during the matinée. It was at this event that Dame Ninette de Valois took one look at the Russian guest and marked him down for the rôle of Albrecht in *Giselle*; in her mind, there was nothing illogical in a partnership with Fonteyn, and the latter was soon enough persuaded that she could either join in – or step aside and watch a new ballet phenomenon sweep past her. In the event, unlikely as it was in terms of compatibility, each gave something to the other. Better, each challenged the other. Across a divide of generation and background, some mainspring of common purpose was tapped – almost overnight. News of the pairing had caused ticket queues to form days before that first booking season opened. Perhaps it was a natural adjunct of the Sixties Revolution: the new openness, the faith in "happenings"; whatever the reason, expectation was high in London, with 70,000 disappointed subscribers. Artistically, the risks were considerable. On the evening of February 21, 1962, the partnership was launched; the general opinion

was "poetic magic". At the final curtain, lucky ticket holders rose as one, shouting their praise during countless curtain calls; and within days, Nureyev joined the company in the same capacity as Fonteyn: Permanent Guest Artist. De Valois saw him as a vital challenge for the Royal's younger male dancers.

Fonteyn was interested in examining all aspects of the production of *Giselle* afresh; she had, after all, a chance to compare the versions she had learned from St. Petersburg dancers such as Tamara Karsavina, with a modern alumnus from the same school. Nureyev proved to be impatient with some of the traditional mime sections, long since abandoned by the Kirov company in Leningrad, but he found also that much of the London patterning still meshed exactly with the versions he had grown up with. Fonteyn enjoyed the full-blooded Romantic colour which Nureyev invested in Albrecht, and showed herself ready to rethink some of her own traditional interpretation as a result. Although she was deeply fond of the ballet, she was aware too that opinions were more than usually divergent as to her success with the rôle of Giselle; many fellow dancers were in great awe of her interpretation, while some segments of public opinion wondered why she persisted with a ballet that did not obviously favour her natural strengths. As usual, she enjoyed the challenge and persisted with the work, and many subsequent performances with Nureyev reached the greatest heights of poetic suggestion. In all, she managed over thirty years in this ballet, and only gave it

up with reluctance. Ironically, it was a stage accident in the same work which hastened the decision. In Portugal, the lid of a property barrel was not secured firmly when Fonteyn was lifted onto it, in the harvest scene. She went through with a crash, giving one knee a serious blow in the process. Though she concealed the matter, the physical aggravation from this injury caused problems for years afterwards.

Swan Lake was the next major ballet to be re-examined by the Fonteyn-Nureyev partnership. Here, too, Nureyev was impatient with some of the old mime passages, but Fonteyn was less inclined to be swayed over a ballet she had mastered in so profound a manner for so many years. In the history of ballet no other dancer had performed so many versions, so many times; her first performance in the dual rôle had been three months before Nureyev was born. Working with such an exemplar, he soon enough acknowledged that she was right to stick to her reading of the work. "It is your best rôle – and you *are* the best." This accolade did not prevent him mounting an entirely new production of the ballet in Vienna, wherein Nureyev choreography replaced almost all of the revered Petipa and Ivanov configurations. Fonteyn cheerfully learned yet another version, and the two dancers were greeted with phenomenal acclaim. It is said that the curtain calls after the opening night's performance constituted a new world record, and subsequently both dancers were depicted on a postage stamp. Around this time, Fonteyn (who was partnered by numerous other leading male dancers) was performing in four distinctly different versions of *Swan Lake* in as many weeks, with two productions abroad, and two in England. One of the latter had a particularly beautiful last act re-choreographed by Ashton, and this showed Fonteyn's elegiac quality to perfection. For her, it must have been like a pianist having four entirely different versions of fingering, for one concerto.

At the time of her fiftieth birthday, she was performing *Swan Lake* (with the Royal Ballet) in New York, where audiences and critics alike were lost in admiration at her continuing control of the ballet, not least the pyrotechnics of Act Three, where they spoke of "adamantine brilliance". As always, she was resigned to performing the 32 fouettés as an act of sheer determination, for they had never been less than a bugbear, but she was usually able to conceal these worries from the public; and elsewhere, under Nureyev's constant exhortations, she could produce passages of technical brilliance that might have been beyond her in younger days. By now there was an acceptance of the fact that, after such a standard, performances could only dwindle, yet Fonteyn retained sufficient flexibility that, combined with her unrivalled sense of style and presentation, younger audiences felt exhilaration and not disappointment at her appearances. Her general physical appearance was entirely beguiling in this respect, and many onlookers were often incredulous at her reported age – a fact she never took the slightest pains to avoid. Often, she would appear in New York in a spring

With Nureyev in Paradise Lost, *1967.*

season, on or around her birthday, and she looked forward to the younger elements in the audience singing her Happy Birthday. No ballerina could have been more genuinely adored by her public, and the demonstrations of that regard were often deeply touching. It was as Aurora in *The Sleeping Beauty* that she set the greatest standards for her successors. Over more than thirty years, her portrayal of the rôle became an archetypal template against which all other contenders were compared. Ironically, it was far from being her favourite work. From the time when she was first pitched into the hugely demanding technicalities of the rôle, Fonteyn realised there was nowhere to hide. To her chagrin, she discovered that the dramatic tone was almost nonexistent in the character: a happy sixteen-year-old princess. On this bare outline she had to sketch a portrait that could sustain herself, as well as the audience. Early on, she conceived a positive hatred for the solo to the violin variation in the first act, and her distaste for its fussiness never left her; but onlookers knew none of this; they were captivated by the charm, the delicacy, the precision. All over the world they cheered; this image of girlhood set by Petipa and Tchaikowsky in 1890, and embodied afresh by Fonteyn, fifty years later. This work, too, she danced for over thirty years. When she was fifty-two, she agreed to appear with Nureyev in performances of *The Sleeping Beauty* in Marseilles. Somehow, she was announced for four performances in three days; even in the toughest days of the war she had never attempted such a thing. Rather than let down the

French audience, she risked an evening performance straight after a matinée, and sailed through another three acts, with total aplomb. As Nureyev said later, "You never see anything like it. Ever!"

It was generally agreed that the progression between a Fonteyn dress rehearsal and a first performance could be huge, and the increase in nuance and definition between first and second performances just as marked. She refined her rôles on stage, constantly, through the repetition of them, and she explored more than eighty rôles in her extraordinary career. Her range in all these ballets was almost limitless; the shy, forlorn flower-girl in *Nocturne*; flamboyant Success, in *The Wanderer*; the mysterious cat-girl of *Les demoiselles de la nuit*; the flashing, inhuman Firebird; gentle Cinderella; spirited Chloë; seductive Ondine; the dippy society girl in *Façade*; the implacable Péri; the breathtakingly elegant Merry Widow. This rôle call, from common farce to high tragedy, was given spirited life during thirty-five years non-stop performing. Thirty years after she had last danced the flower girl in *Nocturne*, she put on the costume again, for an appearance in a gala to honour Sir Frederick Ashton. The dress still fitted as securely as the part, and those members of the audience who had seen her all those years earlier were transfixed by the sight; to them it was as if some spell swept away the intervening years; nothing had altered. Those seeing the simple little solo for the first time found their view unaccountably misted by tears. Elsewhere in the evening, Chloë, Marguerite, and

As Paquita.

the Woman in the Ballgown, from *Apparitions*, were seen fresh minted, while the delicate shapes from *The Wise Virgins* reminded everyone of the way Ashton exploited the Fonteyn arms.

Today, 'line' in ballet is in danger of becoming a lost art. Fonteyn showed that the mathematical possibilities in this department could be almost limitless in terms of colour and weight; given half a chance choreographically, she would 'score' a part so that the eye was fed a stream of equations that would somehow hang about in the mind, like a series of wonderful carvings; and these would often 'play' to some linear element of adjacent décor, as well. (The picture opposite demonstrates this characteristic.) Musicians sometimes said she could make the score visible. She hated the idea of counting beats when learning a rôle; she said it prevented her from hearing the music, and the better the music was played, the more she forgot about the difficult steps. She absorbed the characteristics of different nationalities in their way of movement and gesture; it was said that in Paris, her Aurora was a French girl; in Tokyo it was scaled more demurely. Her successes in foreign lands were never compromised by the archaic vocabulary of her art; each audience (if reviews are to be half believed) felt she spoke directly to them, in a language they found entirely personal. In France, they likened her to a well-planted flower, renewing itself afresh as each season arrived. In Australia, they thought her like a great Test batsman, "always in the right position at the right moment, always seeming to have time to spare". Others thought she embodied the best principles of jazz, finding the centre of a musical line and then shifting the weight back and forth at will, while never missing the path. Whatever she did, it was done without fuss or fanfare, quietly and determinedly, to the best of her ability. The result was that her pre-eminence was never seriously questioned, once people began to absorb the variety of her accomplishments, and she was one of the most enduring of great theatrical stars, in an age cluttered with ephemeral ones. Within an art form that is cruelly demanding, she continually made the difficult appear easy and the complex seem natural, and seemed able, always, to turn her present into her prime, so that other stars of the theatre always flocked to see whatever she did. Like Anna Pavlova, her global forays were statistically breathtaking. She carried a simple enough message: that dancing is enjoyable. Above all, she danced with love, and for that, the love was returned wherever she went.

Despite her continual quest for an appearance of simplicity, shaving off the fuss and trimmings, Fonteyn's means to this end were many-layered. Even her miraculously harmonious line was, mathematically speaking, extremely complex. Beyond the stage, her naturalness of manner did combine many elements: reticence, humour, and no-nonsense application; but right there is something of a juggling act. Amongst her inborn qualities, paramount was sheer bravery, which got her through things that

Ophelia, in Hamlet.

would have defeated most people. She quite enjoyed tussling with problems; she could be like a terrier with a stick over some matters, and a challenge was better than a good meal, for Margot. Although she hated to rationalise her performances with reconstruction and motivation, she did have exactly the sort of mind suited to it, and it must have been going on at a deeply subconscious level, perhaps quite unbidden. (After a particularly good cinema film, she was quite capable of walking around for an hour or more, analysing the motivations of some character.) On stage, she made things look as if they 'just happened', yet they always happened at the right millisecond, on the right day; she had a phenomenal ability to deliver as required, and in that situation she was totally aware, every second. One morning, after a remarkable performance of *Swan Lake* the previous night, I said to Rudolf Nureyev, "Now, there you are! Even *you* have to agree, that was a *perfect performance*, last night." He nodded agreement; in itself, an unusual admission; then he added, rather wistfully, "I know. But I can't do all that concentration, like Margot. It exhausts me too much." The implication was that, having attempted it the previous night, the degree of extra energy required had unnerved him somewhat. This seems to get us to the core of the Fonteyn strength.

Margot's great excellence in some ways made her almost a victim: of the expectations of so many people, far and wide, and this pressure was compounded by her deep-seated aversion to doing anything at all

not well. The fact is, she led a totally unnatural life; even in childhood, there was always some *force majeure* at work, ensuring she was not really like other people, at all. When she married, that pattern continued; her private life was often as bizarre as any ballet plot, and sometimes it required a great Fonteyn performance to hide the fact. But that, too, was handled with a combination of fortitude and consummate skill, and the whole seems a very difficult act for anyone to contemplate following.

We must assume she had the fears that mortals have, yet she always concealed them immaculately. When she arrived first at the Vic-Wells Ballet and encountered de Valois, she was in her own words, "really very frightened of her." This, she felt in retrospect, was a very good thing. "If you don't have that sort of discipline when you are young, you cannot cope when you are older." In her work, some rôles frightened her – quite markedly, if one believes her own telling of it. One can see this sort of theatrical fear crush some performers, but with Margot the fear was always put to work; she would advance steadily towards the eye of the storm with no perceptible tremor. This inimitable quality may even have lulled her audiences slightly, since there was no possibility of her being erratic. Her attributes have been endlessly analysed: the inbuilt sense of discipline; the intuitive and complex musicality; the all-pervading measure; the sunny disposition. All these elements played their part in her development, and indeed in her subsequent survival. As with any dancer, there were times when she felt she was losing the way (in her own words, "clinging on by my eyelashes,") but at those times her willpower invariably pulled her through - and then, she set about finding a way to improve. (When she first heard her own voice she was appalled, and immediately set about altering the pitch.)

Margot herself, in later life, elected to say that nobody could really remember why she first went to ballet lessons. This post-entry overlooked her own mother's comments published in one of Margot's own books, *A Dancer's World*, written for potential students and their parents. In it, Mrs. Hookham contributed a parental view, detailing the circumstances of Margot's early progress. It is an admirable item, and to read it afresh is to hear precisely the voice of Mrs. Hookham – from whom, incidentally, Margot must have inherited her wonderfully ordered and concise phraseology. "We lived in Ealing when I took her to her first ballet class. Her father in fact suggested the classes would be good for her deportment, which to me seemed an extraordinary word to use, because although, when she was concentrating on a game or trying to read, she would hunch her shoulders and screw up her eyes, her body was as straight as a young sapling." Margot's father never questioned his daughter's lithe grace, but he was keen to see it safeguarded. He told me that the whole subject only arose because Margot/Peggy had a tendency to slide down a chair, whenever she was at table. (Possibly when faced with one of the many foods she declined to eat. The image of that perfect carriage makes it seem unlikely – and yet the mind governs the body, and her food fads *were* quite extreme.)

Margot's own entertaining account of her childhood years paints a picture, wittingly or not, of a placid yet exceptionally determined child, in some ways old before her time. I know that when she was still very young, one of her aunts remarked one day, "I am sure Peggy has been here many times before." Her mother felt she had a natural, inborn control. Given the circumstances, it is valid to wonder if the child was immutably cast in the adult rôle. I suspect that she was, and I think, too, that Margot, deep down, also felt this; which is why she was always at pains to make expressions of surprise about her success. Diligence in the pursuit of an objective did not entirely accord with her belief that one should never take oneself too seriously, and it made her uncomfortable to encounter the immoderate seriousness with which many people attended her every move. The current of acclaim that bore her forward could very easily have upended her, but she was saved by her great sense of proportion. The irony, in her case, was that she was destined from an early age to become important, in herself, for countless other people, and she spent the greater part of her life trapped in this expectation. Because she always went to some pains to conceal any hint of ambition in her make-up, the 'happy chance' syndrome coloured her own reminiscences, yet there was always a degree of purpose lurking there – at *some* level.

As soon as the young Peggy had attended her first dancing classes, aged four, there was no stopping her. Her mother once said to me, "She wouldn't want it said, now, but if anyone was being dragged kicking and screaming, I was!" The great luck was in that first teacher, back in the London suburb of Ealing. Grace Bosustow was a teacher accredited by the Association of Operatic Dancing (later the Royal Academy of Dancing), and the precepts by which she taught were strictly defined and adjudged to be physically sage for each age group. About Margot, Miss Bosustow's retrospective view was that "she had the most perfect grace I have ever seen in an untrained child. From the first I thought she was a sweet little girl and very original. Though I don't think she was shy in the usual sense of the word, she seldom spoke unless spoken to, and would never say 'Yes' if a nod would do as well. Her manner was very grave and somehow remote. She was not at all vivacious, and everything she did was placid and determined." Less publicised has been the reaction of Miss Bosustow's niece (who may have been conscious of a rival); for her, Peggy Hookham was "a grim little thing – a black-eyed Susan, and not a child you'd look at twice except for the neatness of her." Inevitably, it was Peggy who was chosen to lead eight other children onto the stage in a number called *The Little Co-Optimists*. Peggy was just five, but was given the honour because "she was absolutely reliable." For another school matinée, Peggy was given an Irish jig to perform. Miss Bosustow, on her way shopping prior to the concert, happened to glance over the hedge of the Hookham front garden and was surprised to see Peggy practising determinedly by herself. "She really practised, going over the same step over and over again . . . very unusual for so young a child."

In that year, 1924, the *Middlesex County Times* reviewed the children's efforts: "In the *Silver Ballet* there was a remarkably fine solo dance by Peggy Hookham, which was vigorously encored." No surprise there; however, behind the scenes, matters were never quite so untroubled. Peggy suffered from anticipatory nerves and fears which invariably induced a fever exactly forty-eight hours before any competition, and to this was added the complications of her being a bad traveller; there was always the image of Peggy sitting in the back seat of the motor car, huddled, silent, and green in the face. She was never less than thoroughly miserable before any childhood dance events, and only her toy rabbit, Week, could provide solace at such times.

Week went everywhere. The name arose from the plaintive and squeaky voice first given him as his proxy, by Mrs. Hookham. This transfer of vocals was taken up by the child, and whenever she felt unable to express herself on some matter, Week would be made to step in. 'Week says this'. 'Week says the other'. Under this system, Week's mistress could go for long periods without having to express a direct opinion on anything at all. Even when the dancing classes had started, Week was still the principal

Washington, DC.

spokesman on general matters, and if Mrs. Hookham wished to give her daughter a small catechism on dance matters, then she had to pick her moment, perhaps when Peggy was occupied in helping her mother with some household task, minus Week.

"I bet you don't know what a plié is?"

"Yes, I do."

"Go on – I bet you don't really know, you're only saying that."

"Yes I *do*! A plié is a bending of the knees over the toes."

Peggy's intractable streak was seldom overcome by direct confrontation. In grade examinations for Miss Bosustow's class, she gained Honours in the first, second and third grades, and missed them in the fourth only because of one incorrect answer. "I knew I was wrong, the moment I said it," she reported afterwards, "but I wouldn't go back on it." The dichotomy that existed between Peggy's view of dance exams, and her attitude toward her school exams, was extreme. Her father told me once that the school variety held no terrors for his daughter. With a chuckle, he suddenly recalled walking her across Ealing Common for some important day at an early school, and Peggy bursting out with, "Oh Daddy, I do *like* exams. You never know whether you are going to come out the top, or the bottom!" (That was surely the adult talking, right there on the common.)

In her early years, Peggy had one idol: her brother, and she was a willing slave for any of his endeavours

Peggy deferring to Week.

34

in which she was allowed to participate. As Felix had inherited his father's mechanical turn of mind, he was forever constructing gadgets, and Peggy, on endless search and carry missions, soon earned a family nickname of The Fitter's Mate. Their nursery was at the very top of their home, so that Peggy spent much of her second year, at least, labouring up four flights of stairs of her knees, and then bottom-bouncing down again with the object of her mission. As they progressed in their childhood, the brother and sister established a warm relationship, much of it sheer romping fun, and Peggy showed no great inclination to establish friends outside the family circle. Her initial education was via a governess who taught a group of five children locally, and Peggy was the only girl in the group. This fitted in with her perceived order of things; by her own telling she had no great knack for gaining the confidence of other little girls, and never went out of her way to try. Significantly, her mother once said of the young Margot, "she could never stand to be number two in anything." Of course, in the company of her brother, or other boys, she was *hors concours*, which suited her admirably.

Her mother had a clear-eyed and unsentimental view of her daughter's capacities, and always took care to understand what, exactly, the child's teachers were implanting. Once she had acquired that knowledge, she then tried to inculcate the same message, and this constancy must have been invaluable for a quick learner. Mrs. Hookham's own good fortune was in having a relatively free domestic regime, allowing her time to attend the dancing classes very often - which Miss Bosustow did not discourage. The mother had the wisdom never to comment on what she saw there. Privately, she too thought that Peggy was unquestionably a better mover than the others; doing the same movements, "she just looked different." When Mr. Hookham's work dictated a move to China (via America), Mrs. Hookham was able to monitor potential tuition and effectively avoid pitfalls. After one class, in Kentucky, she could announce firmly, "We won't be going *there* again!" It was the sort of problem still worrying Anna Pavlova, who spent countless hours on her world travels counselling against hasty and incorrect schooling, which could ruin young talent.

Peggy's separation from her brother was the first serious emotional dislocation in her life, but she had the distractions of widespread foreign travel, which gave her an early understanding of the sheer diversity of life. Following periods in Tientsin, and Hong Kong, the family then settled in Shanghai, and Mrs. Hookham resumed her hunt for suitable dance tuition for Peggy. Of three Russian teachers, Mrs. Hookham had a sufficient ground knowledge of the rights and wrongs of schooling that she was able instantly to weed out an injurious member of the trio; another case of "We won't be going *there* again!" She did approve of George Gontcharov, a former Bolshoi student. He recognised in Peggy what he described as "a ballerina's head. Her face seemed to talk to me. She held herself beautifully. She was always somehow intent, as though she had some idea that she knew what she was about." Under the guidance of Gontcharov, Peggy soon enough discovered that there could be more to ballet than its difficult and seemingly dry exercises.

By the time Peggy was ten, apart from a short-lived enthusiasm for riding, absolutely no other interests beckoned. The child knew that she could express herself in movement, and that expression was somehow fulfilling. School had become ordinary, and dancing somehow extraordinary. While schoolbooks may have seemed unenticing, other pages were devoured with enthusiasm; these were English theatrical magazines, and the stage dance sections were the subject of much discussion, with Peggy quite unusually voluble; indeed, if this self-sufficient child learned that some other English child had actually been to the theatre, in London, then her interest was suddenly intense, and the other child would probably be subjected to a grilling on every aspect of the event. It was this evident passion that eventually convinced the mother that if it was to be furthered sensibly, then a vital decision would have to be made, about returning to London. In effect, Mrs. Hookham at this point put her daughter's potential career some degree ahead of her own marriage. It seems that Mr. Hookham reacted philosophically; though he was not in a position to change the course of his own career, still, he could see that it was unrealistic to imagine that China could be the happiest environment for an English teenager. Indeed, amongst their friends, Mrs. Bear and her daughter June were already booked on a ship for England, to further June's ambitions in dancing, and faced with this competitive element, the Hookham family decided to match the challenge. So the die was cast and, in effect, at this moment the child had won.

Somewhere in my stores there is film footage of Margot taken in the old Pheasantry studio in the King's Road, before the principal structure was demolished. I had heard the story of Margot's first visit there in some detail, from her mother, and so it was fascinating to take Margot back to the building in 1968, to film her as she moved around the room remembering incidents and personalities from thirty five years earlier. She had not been back to the building since 1934. The combination of her mother's memories, and her own, made a vivid impression. When Mrs. Hookham took her daughter back to London from Shanghai in 1933, they faced a huge psychological hurdle trying to get the fourteen-year-old Peggy taken seriously by reputable dance instructors, since their terms of reference were practically non-existent. Mrs. Hookham had singled out the Princess Seraphine Astafieva because she had been the teacher of Alicia Markova; but getting an audience was extremely hard going, and there were a number of letters and telephone calls before the nerve-making first appointment. The Pheasantry was a bizarre enough framework for this encounter; the entrance (which still survives) was an arched por-

Outdoor class,
South of France.

tico surmounted by triumphant Roman figures; beyond this, cushioned from the Chelsea traffic, one went through a Moorish forecourt, then along a gloomy and narrow hallway, before stumbling up a dark half-turn of stairs to reach a big oak-panelled doorway; this was genuine Georgian. The studio beyond was, for a painter, huge. During the princess's tenure, it had been fitted out with barres and mirrors, in the usual way, but the little ante rooms were dark and mysteriously lit, with heavy Russian curtains pulled across the windows. There was also incense, and the patterned drapes glinted and winked because their flower patterns were inset with little pieces of mirror which played back the reflected light, and the soft glow of two lights burning beneath an ikon. When we went back there again, in the sixties, Margot's first instinct was to see if the floor still squeaked; she remembered this from their first entrance, when they had followed Vera (Madame's assistant, Verishka) to meet Astafieva. In the eyes of Peggy in 1933, it was the Balkan Sobranie cigarette curling smoke at the end of a long ivory holder which marked out the woman sitting in an armchair as a true ballerina. Margot in her autobiography paints a precise picture of those early classes with Astafieva, but in point of fact the princess did not accept Peggy simply on the strength of Mrs. Hookham's desperate argument: that she had brought her daughter all the way from Shanghai with the sole purpose of studying with Astafieva. Margot's version lets it seem that this notion was enough to get her accepted, but there was actually the further hurdle of an audition

the following Monday, alongside a boy who took private lessons.

During the brief initial interview, Peggy had not spoken a word, of course, but sat in her customary silence watching the encounter between her mother and this exotic and melancholic lady with her black dress and her pink bandeau. On the Monday of the audition they found Madame in a full black skirt, with white cotton stockings and black buttoned shoes. An entirely shapeless sweater was enlivened by a long string of pearls, yet it was only the inevitable cigarette holder, plus a scarf tied like a turban, which really redressed the balance in favour of the 'ballerina image' that Peggy had come to expect. Astafieva gave Mrs. Hookham a courtly nod and then asked the young man already in the studio whether he minded her inspecting "this child" while they worked. An old lady pianist played from a corner of the studio. It was only at the very end of the class that Astafieva gave a clue to her reaction. Turning to Mrs. Hookham she said, "All right! She can come! She needs private lessons every day, and she must come to the bigger classes too." Then came the words that carried the most import of all. "The fees will be a guinea a class."

The cost of these lessons with Astafieva was such that Mrs. Hookham had to exercise the strictest forms of budgeting, and mother and daughter needed to devise all sorts of stringent economies to get by. At first they were lodged in a women's club, but later

Indoor class, South of France.
In this picture, one can perhaps see Peggy Hookham practising in the garden in Ealing, forty years earlier. Also, it is a rare glimpse of the no-nonsense Margot, whom one would not challenge unless one was very sure of one's ground – or else very foolhardy.

Mrs. Hookham was able to find a mews flat. This had an attic space reached by ladder, and there Peggy was able to practice some of the class sequences, and criticise her own positions, with the help of an old over-mantel mirror which they had propped against the end wall. Despite the difficulties, it was all thought to be worthwhile, as Peggy quickly fell under the influence of Astafieva's regal authority, and accepted all the work with her usual diligence. She soon came to adore this remote lady who never dispensed praise in so many words, but who still had the knack of letting her pupils know when she was pleased. It was not so long after Peggy had begun the classes at The Pheasantry that Astafieva one day asked Verishka which pupil she considered the most promising. Verishka replied, "The little dark one is the one to watch." She was impressed with the strength and neatness of the student from Shanghai, "like a young, well-trained pony."

When, after six months, Mrs. Hookham decided that Peggy should go for an audition with the Vic-Wells Ballet, this idea was greeted with alarm by the student herself. "I'm not *nearly* ready!" It was to become a frequent cry. By now, she hated any idea of leaving Astafieva, who had begun to help her understand the magical quality of Theatre that can lie behind the simplest movements and gestures. Astafieva's own response to the suggestion had been "If *I* say she is ready, she is ready." But she did concede that Peggy should probably try for an audition with Ninette de Valois' group in Islington. There,

she was accepted for the Sadler's Wells school, and at the end of ten weeks there was a big day for the Hookham household when a postcard arrived: "Peggy Hookham will attend *corps de ballet* rehearsals for *Casse-Noisette* – Snowflakes." The child with the bad feet had been approved for public viewing, at least at snowflake level. Peggy was thrilled; a stage career beginning, and two shillings and sixpence for each performance. Mrs. Hookham was less convinced by all this and felt that de Valois might have been desperate for snowflakes of any standing. Not entirely convinced that a true career was awaiting her daughter, she sought an audience with Miss de Valois, and asked her, "Would you mind telling me what you think of Peggy? I know she could be a very good character dancer, but..." A shriek of mirth from de Valois cut her short. "Character dancer! Character dancer? Do you hear what she says? A character dancer!" This response so baffled Mrs. Hookham that de Valois had quickly to check her merriment and say seriously, "She will be a classical dancer." Mrs. Hookham did not at first take in the nuance, and so bowled on. "It's no good me spending all this money if she's no good, or if she's only going to be a back-row girl. I'd like to know!" De Valois then looked at her squarely, before saying, "My dear, *no* money you spend on that child will be wasted. So far as I know, unless anything happens to her, she has a great future." When Mrs. Hookham gave me a graphic replay of this interview, all those years later, she then added, "But that was de Valois – who was *a very wise woman.*"

Acknowledging public response – including a bouquet larger than herself – after Raymonda Act Three, Athens, 1963.

…and in Ambleteuse, France, 1922

With Felix, in Troon (and already the prey of cameras)…

…where she is showing an early accommodation with the sea.

The child

*The tambourine lady who earned an
encore, and a comment in the press, in 1924.*

With the watchman's daughter, Tientsin, 1927.

In the bund area of the Russian Concession, Tientsin – and already complaining about being trapped by the camera, because she is not free to arrange herself harmoniously, within 'the scene'.

Taken in Bideford in Devon in 1927, (prior to the first voyage to China) with Felix, and his schoolfriend, Philip. In this picture, a dancing instructor would notice the wonderfully straight legs, and anyone who knew the adult Margot would recognise the 'I don't want to!' expression, which has arisen, in this situation, because Peggy is confined to the breakwater and has no room to manoeuvre herself into a more characteristic contrapuntal position (as with the rabbit, opposite).

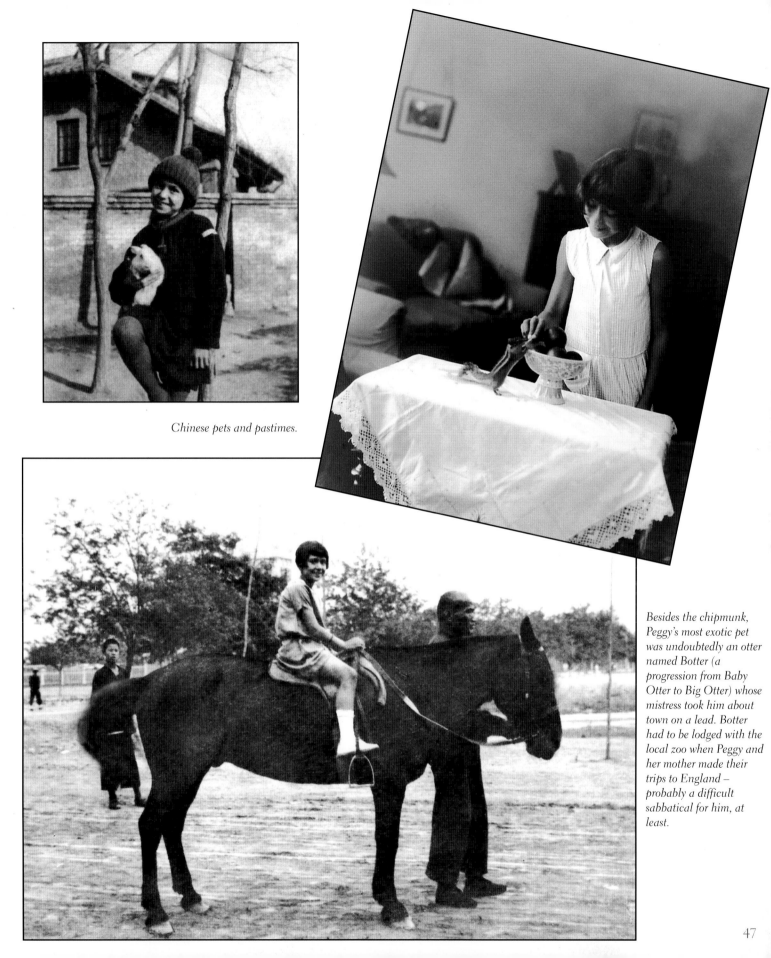

Chinese pets and pastimes.

Besides the chipmunk, Peggy's most exotic pet was undoubtedly an otter named Botter (a progression from Baby Otter to Big Otter) whose mistress took him about town on a lead. Botter had to be lodged with the local zoo when Peggy and her mother made their trips to England – probably a difficult sabbatical for him, at least.

47

With her parents, in the Repulse Bay Hotel in Hong Kong in 1929, when Peggy
spent six months free of dance classes – and almost perpetually in the sea. This
period of intense swimming, at this particular age, may well have set the Fonteyn
'line' in the calf, which, with its remarkably smooth profile, was idiosyncratic
for a dancer.

Felix's first proper portrait of his sister, taken on Ealing Common during
a 1930 English sabbatical. The spot now lies deep under a motorway.

Giselle

From her earliest days in *Giselle*, at least from the time when she had overcome her terror of appearing at all, Fonteyn actively enjoyed the stage experience of this ballet, in ways which never lessened over three decades. She became innured to the few voices who said she was 'too this', or 'too that' for the rôle; some thread running through this ballet fascinated and supported her. I can recall looking at a new booking schedule, in the mid-sixties, while Margot was in the room, and seeing *Giselle* listed (it was never my favourite) I burst out with, "Oh – not Giselle *again!*" Herself took this bêtise in good spirit, and cocked her head on one side and thought a while, and then said, "Oh, I don't know. There's something about that old ballet." She did, I suspect, readily identify with the character's unswerving devotion; and I think, equally, she knew what it was to be deceived or betrayed. She identified too with the steadfast qualities which Giselle embodies; and even if it meant a black and white world, right versus wrong, with Giselle herself seeming a bit dippy, then after all, it was this extreme of innocence and oddness which caught the attention of a prince obviously well versed in knowingness and concealment. When she first took on the rôle, Margot was always fascinated by the way Robert Helpmann could stoke up the audience's involvement, right from his first entry. Backstage, awaiting her own entry, she could feel the cone of the audience's attention tighten its focus, as soon as Helpmann came on from the prompt side, opposite. With everything having been wound up a notch or two, opening the cottage door was, for Margot, almost like opening a gift box: there was something just begging to be discovered. When she darted around, listening for signal sounds from the hiding Albrecht, this Giselle was delightedly aiming her little charade directly at her concealed admirer; her fun was innocent, yet also coquettish.

Because of her general excitability, this Giselle was also quick to tears when imagining that Albrecht had retreated; however, with the game of the plucked petals, with its potential for being upsetting, here she seemed so certain that he really loved her, that any "he loves me not" petals were scarcely portentous. And with the dances involving Albrecht, and the harvesters, Fonteyn's Giselle had a vivacity which quickly whipped up a general gaiety. She was far from being shy; as the measures progressed, so she abandoned herself to the fun of it all, robustly; no wonder she made her mother watchful. This 'one of the gang' good humour may have disquieted some members of the critical fraternity expecting to see Giselle embodying all the hallmarks of a creature apart, but Margot was always careful to play Giselle in Act One according to her own spirits – that is, as a forthright and uncomplicated soul. Not for her a maiden so self-absorbed as to be highlighting her own frailties. Of course, the strictures of a mother, so determined to put a stop to all this potential over-

"If you carry on like this, you will die!"

Equally, the princess's shattering disclosure: that the playboy Albrecht is really betrothed to her, brought forth an almost confrontational situation. Fonteyn's Giselle had no mind for rank or deference, once this point had been reached; this was where right or wrong, black or white, took over, and even a princess might – indeed, must – be wrong. The intervention of the self-justifying Hilarion, with the damning evidence of the princely sword he has found concealed in the woodcutter's hut, provides the perfect theatrical hook – what Hitchcock would have called the macguffin. For the Fonteyn Giselle, this evidence pitched her cruelly off the ledge of her happy right world into a blackly wrong world almost of an instant; she no longer recognised her surroundings or familiars. Her world was turned upside down and her balance was thrown, so that in treading on the discarded sword at one point, she could not see it for what it was, but must needs crouch like a blind person to feel the outline, for an identity. Then, when she drew the circle with the sword, it was with a new spirit of intent, almost glee, and the cabalistic overtones would be sufficient reason for the villagers to become doubly concerned. Was Giselle somehow possessed?

exertion, would come the harder to a girl who had never pursued artful decorum, so that when she finally hears from the mother the doom scenario, about a congenitally weak heart, it provokes a positive, almost defiant response from the girl. Her heart? How ridiculous to question the strength of *her* heart!

With the evidence of the prince's deception,
Giselle's world is shattered.

Giselle suddenly recognises her mother and starts
towards her –but she never reaches her.

The exact moment when Giselle's heart fails…

Over the years, Margot had listened to all the reasonings about the *ballet blanc* aspects of Act Two: its historic formula, but she always found the shift in gear between the two acts uncomfortably wide. Modern audiences will not accept a Giselle who expires gracefully and with porcelain prettiness at the end of Act One; they want an element of the visceral; and twenty minutes after this heart-tugging collapse, the same girl must spring around with the strength of a leopard – which is visually contradictory. Margot lived with the knowledge that she wasn't a jumper, in the athletic sense; her aerial qualities came more from suggestion (at which she was immensely skilled) and to disguise her lack of a big jump, she developed a cantilena flow that had the effect of creating a long-spanning arc through the choreography, in the manner of a finely-crafted suspension bridge. She 'flew', through phrasing. As for her interpretation of who – or what – Giselle was: this spirit somehow made visible at midnight, she saw her part more as an idea than an entity; her rôle was to embody the idealism of true love, and its potential for redemption. She was the token, that Albrecht, as the survivor, could turn over a new leaf and go on to lead a fulfilling life. In the partnership with Nureyev, this concept worked very powerfully; it was as if Giselle had transferred a flame of hope to the repentant mortal; and when she faded back into her woodland grave, that was the irreversible extinction of Giselle. Mission accomplished.

Because of the strength of tradition which does linger and support (or should) different ballet generations, particularly in relation to exemplar rôles in the major classics, I should probably record here a *Giselle* anecdote. In the twenties, opinion had apparently divided over two outstanding interpretors of the title rôle: on the one hand were those who declared that Anna Pavlova's reading was unearthly, and sacrosanct, (and it became the template for Markova's performances); on the other, were advocates of Pavlova's potential rival, Olga Spessivtseva who, they felt, presented fresh nuances, enhanced by her strong yet delicate physique. Spessivtseva's career, interrupted by mental imbalance, had itself become the stuff of legend by the sixties. Anton Dolin's discovery of one of his former dance partners, residing in a mental institution, and his successful efforts to reintegrate her with the outside world, became well-known when he published a book about the saga.

In the spring of 1965, Margot had joined the Royal Ballet's New York season nursing two separate injuries – yet under intense pressure from the impresario to stick to the schedule. Within a week of her arrival, she also developed a bad cough which soon went deep into her lungs. The doctors diagnosed the first stages of pleurisy. Not unmindful of Pavlova's ultimate fate due to this condition, I for one was deeply concerned at Margot's willingness to go on in *Giselle*; it seemed horribly risky, both for her health, and indeed her reputation, if it all went wrong. At this stage, Margot was equally driven by a general fear that if she gave in to 'weakness', or lost her performing rhythm, then her general abilities would spiral out of control and she would never right herself again. This was really her greatest fear. Her domestic life was one of perpetual crisis and alarum, and in truth, much of her continuing equilibrium was cushioned by her stage life; from the moment that she stepped into the wings, the other life was banished for an hour or three, to be replaced by the alternative dramas of that particular ballet's plot. So, she would not be dissuaded about *Giselle*, and she went from doctors' rooms, to dressing room. Some time before curtain up, I popped my head around her door, to see if there was anything she needed, and I found her in a distracted state:
"I don't know whether I can go on. It's terrible!"
"It isn't terrible; everyone will understand. You're allowed an 'off' at least once in a decade."
"What? No – you don't understand. It isn't this," (coughing as she said it,) "it's because Pat Dolin has just sent a note around. He's bringing Spessivtseva! To the performance! I don't know what to do." She stared at herself distractedly in the mirror, and then began scrabbling through the items laid out on her dressing table. The actions were totally out of character, and of course I realised well enough that this was really a Ballet crisis. I couldn't imagine (or perhaps I could) why Pat had been so cruel as to announce his plan prior to the performance; he must have known the effect it would have. At that point, Spessivtseva had not been seen in public for many

Fonteyn and Nureyev, Act Two.

years, so any appearance would be heavy with resonance – but as to it being a performance of *Giselle*, with the current assoluta in the rôle, quelle épreuve! At this juncture, I left the dressing room on some mission, and in the very narrow corridor outside I found at that moment two figures approaching from the other end; in front, a trim little figure in a plain wool coat and a small fur hat, and half hidden behind, some silver-haired man in a camel-hair coat. Pressing myself to the wall to let the lady past, I then discovered the man to be Dolin – which made the lady Spessivtseva!

"We've just popped in to see Margot."

No single word formed in my mouth.

With the knowledge of all this, watching the actual performance was incredibly nerve-wracking. There was no calamity on stage. Act One was not one of Margot's best, but Act Two had many of her inimitable touches, and it all drew an ecstatic response from the crowd. Later, Margot admitted that, for much of Act One, she could not feel anything below her knees. "I had *no* idea where the floor was. I was just guessing where my feet might be. I sometimes found myself quite surprised, that I hadn't tripped over them!" After this, by degrees, the pleurisy was somehow shrugged off, and she never missed a scheduled performance. I suppose it might be said that, if she could survive dancing *Giselle* with Spessivtseva watching, then any medical problems were relatively small beer.

La Bayadère

There seems to be no obvious reason why, in The Kingdom of the Shades act, in *La Bayadère*, the prince and the shade of his lost lover should suddenly enter, carrying a long muslin scarf between them; but if anyone knew that a dense ballet needed a macguffin or two, it was Petipa, and the scarf does very nicely in this respect. Theoretically at least, there is the visual metaphor of something binding these two characters; but for an audience primed to such conventions, the scarf simply signals a circus trick: Pay attention! This could go wrong! Roses, ribbons, bows and arrows ... all these inanimate objects can invest a ballet with a potential *frisson*, by their mere presence. The corps and the three soloists in this white act all have vestigial scarves draping their costumes, linked from wrist to head-dress, and this provides a billowy softness to the ensemble work; but nothing much can get in a tangle, because each scarf has a surreptitious tie, at the elbows.

Nikiya's task is to make the audience marvel at her skill in taking slow balances and turns while also holding onto the end of a scarf, above her head, while Solor makes energetic motions at the other end, suggesting he is manipulating all these skills. His real task is actually to do less than he is suggesting, taking care to control the tension, so as not to pull the ballerina off point. When Nureyev began to rehearse Fonteyn in the Royal Ballet's 1963 production of the white act, he found a ballerina who was immediately interested in the shapes made by the scarf itself, so that she endlessly re-appraised this aspect at rehearsal, working out the exact spots at which she had to clasp the muslin, in order to produce the nicest effect; and when the scarf had to be taut, for support at a turn, then she experimented with different angles and degrees of straightness in her balancing arm, to produce some sort of counterpoint to the scarf's line. After several rehearsals, she confided that she found the Minkus score very ordinary indeed, but by then she had begun to absorb the extraordinary mathematical harmonies of Petipa's choreography, which provides every single dancer in the ballet with non-stop equations requiring fine control – and this complexity kept Margot deeply absorbed; and, as she said, the steps seemed to have the awesome inevitability (and thus profundity) of Bach, in terms of structure, which made poor Minkus' underpinnings pale into insignificance.

Fonteyn's musical awareness was undoubtedly very extraordinary, but its surface manifestations were also very puzzling, because the business of 'music' did not seem to flow on, into her off-duty life, at all. My own view is that she found it too much of a master; she was somehow compelled by it, so that once out of the studio, she felt the need to sever the whip hand. In her home studio, in Talgarth Road, there was a piano, and also a radiogram, but I don't think either of these was much exercised, and the records sitting in the cabinet didn't even fill one shelf. They were a desultory collection with no unifying theme (or indeed import) which I suspect came mainly from other people; either as 'amusing' gifts, or as potential ballet scores offered by potential choroegraphers hoping that Fonteyn might enthuse over their plans. A long shot!

Once, when Margot arrived at my address unexpectedly one morning, it was just after I had put on a record of *Le Tricorne*, and upon hearing a theme filtering out into the hall, she positively flung off her coat and very soon was whirling and dipping around the living room (fortunately large) as the Miller's Wife of Massine's ballet. This was certainly a wonderful bonus, for a weekday morning! When the solo was ended, she dropped onto a sofa, slightly breathless, but in the highest of spirits. "Oh, I used to love doing that! I'm sure I was no good in it, at all, but it was such fun to do!" This tells us that, for Margot, music was mostly an imperative, and one imagines that, if she did not move almost as soon as she first heard a gramaphone record, say, then it was not the right record; and if she did move, then the coffee cups were probably at risk. For her, it may have been more relaxing *not* to have music playing in the home. (When he was first in London, Nureyev complained about exactly this aspect of the Fonteyn address.) The incident with the de Falla music demonstrated, too, that choreography was still safely locked away in her system, even if she had not danced a piece in twenty years.

The first dress rehearsal for La Bayadère *at Covent Garden. Nureyev was here commencing a long personal tradition of ignoring dress requirements on these occasions – to the intense frustration of anyone trying to make a photographic record of the production.*

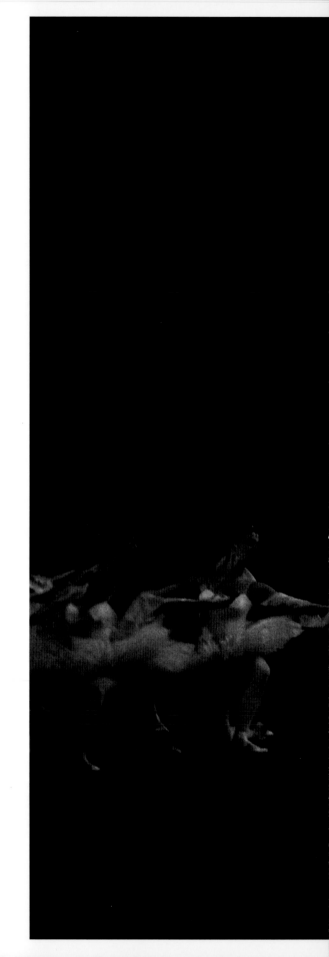

Working out the difficult transition between the high arabesque which turns into the plié pose that follows, immediately after the opening stance of the scarf duet. Nureyev had adapted the man's part, here, to match the ballerina's position, though his hip was not really trained to accomodate such an open extension, thus causing him to force the position at this moment. Here, Fonteyn settled for an exact right-angle, as being more pure than any adjacent angle.

Of course, each ballerina and partner worked out their own fine-tuning with the scarf, and in this respect, there was an evening at Covent Garden when Rudolf, at 'the half', decided he would not be able to manage the ballet, due to an ankle problem, and Christopher Gable was rushed in by taxi, to stand in – though he had never even rehearsed the ballet with Margot. Things went smoothly – until the scarf, when at one moment it dipped a fraction too low and immediately caught in the towering Fonteyn

Early days in La Bayadère *rehearsals, solving the scarf tensions, with Nureyev.*

head-dress – the macguffin here providing its lurking thrill! Another turn, and her head was neatly turbaned. Patrons near the stage could hear Christopher saying, "Don't worry, darling – I'll get you out of it," but at this juncture there was a magnificent 'Fonteyn flourish', almost a frenzy, and Margot somehow cleared it herself. I was sure she had actually stamped her foot during this hiccup, which seemed funny enough to include as a detail in a re-telling of the events, afterwards; at which point Margot all but stamped her foot again. "Don't be ridiculous. Of course I didn't. *That's* how ballet stories start."

When it came to the Nikiya variation in the coda, Nureyev's instruction was very elementary: "Just do diagonal; bit of 'business'." Fonteyn took this calmly, and worked out of thin air a shimmering little exercise of dotted counterpoint, with forward and backward overlapping steps, and a lot of torque in the torso (see page overleaf) – all of which drew no further comment from Rudolf. Both dancers greatly enjoyed the harmonic requirements of the double work in this ballet, which satisfied Margot's deep interest in the basics of classical ballet schooling. She loved the nuances that kept emerging, and would sometimes stop and go over something, adding a faintly different inflexion, in response to an element she had noted in Rudolf, and he in turn would watch out of the corner of his eye everything she was doing. Gradually, the styles would somehow fuse, without either dancer having blurred their individual line, to any obvious extent.

Lebanon: a late afternoon class, and a pause in a night-time rehearsal, at the Baalbek Festival in 1964.

Sometimes, a white owl would float out from one of the upper alcoves, and drift about in its silent, ghostly manner, while a huge melon-coloured moon climbed up into the black velvet sky. It defined the catch-phrase "over the top!" The gigantic Temple of Bacchus and its surrounds (the columns, left, are outside the temple) form one of the most staggeringly impressive antique sites in the world, yet tragically it has been cut off to all visitors for the last 25 years, due to regional and factional conflict.

Athens
This is at a pre-performance rehearsal, on the stage of the Herod Atticus Theatre, with the un-numbered ticket areas already filling, well ahead of time. These early birds have found an interesting selection – not only La Sylphide but also Ashton's Scène d'amour, using Glazunov.
The costume for the sylph (below) has some real 19th-century trickery built into it: at the crucial moment when the sylph is stricken by the witch's poison, the dancer puts a hand to her breast and surreptitiously pulls a release string, at which stroke her wings fall off – most piteously!

Baalbek (right).
A *performance of* Raymonda.

Raymonda

Right from its 1898 première, Russian audiences found the plot of *Raymonda* extremely confusing, and it was said that the storyline of the novel which had inspired it was well nigh impenetrable; (high-born Hungarian lady, betrothed to knight, is abducted by Moorish villain; knight returns from Crusades in time to rescue lady. Question: did lady dream up villain? Indeed, did lady dream up knight?) Yet everyone was swept along by the seemingly inexhaustible invention of Marius Petipa's dance construction, and (the real novelty, this) a rhapsodic new score by Alexander Glazunov, which coursed undiminished through three big acts. Even the dancers said they felt like dancing – an accolade to put Glazunov into the serious Big Time, landing him in the deep footprints of two giants just ahead of him: Leo Delibes and Piotr Tchaikowsky. So, a conjunction of two huge talents, in this instance working carefully in tandem for the preceding two years, got the Tsar's approval (as representing the theatre crowd's opinion) and that got the hinges of the financial coffers re-oiled, and much joy ensued. The poor old storyline, which might so easily have up-ended this otherwise mighty confluence of talent, never did find a rescuer, in the next 100 years, but that lack did not sink the ballet entirely – although the full panoply of all three acts remains a rarity.

If anyone was going to revive *Raymonda*, seriously, in the sixties, it was probably always going to be the Royal Ballet, riding then on a bow wave of public approval, and with huge opera house resources in the background. But when Nureyev suggested the idea to Sir Frederick Ashton (who had previously snipped items from Glazunov's score to support party-pieces for Fonteyn, and for Beriosova) the reaction was negative. Ashton had already struggled to win public approval for three acts of Delibes' *Sylvia*, and he saw *Raymonda* as more of the same problem; at this moment he was also fresh to the job of appeasing a newly adventurous ballet public which happily supported mixed bills (with all the nurturing of varied talent which such programming implies) and he was not keen to be labelled a reactionary, taking up his new post. "Even if it *is* Petipa, that sort of war-horse costs a fortune to mount." During the transitional phase between de Valois and Ashton, the nod went to *La Bayadère's* white act, as being more useful in progressing the general polish of the corps de ballet. Nureyev was undeterred; as soon as he knew that Fonteyn had agreed to lead a Mediterranean and Far East concert tour that summer, he aimed his ideas at her, suggesting a scaled-down version of Act Three as a novelty bravura work. It made sense, and Fonteyn agreed, though there was little time to assemble a company work, or find any costumes which might hint at the Mediaeval.

Even when the 1963 concert group arrived in Athens for the tour's first leg, *Raymonda Act Three* was

hardly assembled; but again, dancers 'just liked it', and as it is easier to work extra time on something that is enjoyable, way past midnight they worked.

The Fonteyn Tour's presentation of Act Three of the ballet was perhaps unexceptional – which was part of its strength; no criticisms filtered back to London, and local opinion was benign; the Mediterranean audiences enjoyed a lush yet unfamiliar score, and anything which showcased the two stars was bound to attract attention. (Indeed, another of Ashton's worries was the ballet becoming labelled a Fonteyn/Nureyev vehicle, with box office repercussions if that pairing did not appear.) Nureyev persisted in his ambition to see all three acts revived, and that autumn he drew into the web of discussions John Field, then director of the Royal's touring section. Field's response was immediately positive; he had a young company eager for challenge, and more than used to hard work, and the idea of Nureyev working with them was a major plus. As for Fonteyn's part in the equation, Field knew all too well the vital importance of a major ballerina occupying the central position, in order to pull the whole mass into focus. His company had recently revived *Sylvia*, and everyone was aware of the strengths and weaknesses of these pantechnicon productions. When the touring company was scheduled to appear in the 1964 Spoleto Festival in Italy, the perfect cue presented itself. Despite continuing reservations filtering through from the Covent Garden board, a deal was struck – although Nureyev

and his ballerina found themselves accountable for certain production costs, particularly costuming. The history of the Spoleto première is chequered (and told elsewhere) but the ballet's success was undoubted. Although Covent Garden relented to accomodate Act Three in its programming, it was left to the burgeoning and ambitious Australian Ballet, with the influence of Robert Helpmann, to see the benefits of an entirely new production of Nureyev's full-length reconstruction. With Fonteyn on board, they roared through England and abroad, to much acclaim, during the 1965/6 winter season.

Two scenes from an early rehearsal in Spoleto.

The second act of Raymonda, *at Baalbek, and Spoleto.*

Raymonda's pas des bouquets *in Act One*
of the Australian Ballet production.

Raymonda's Act Three solo.

With Nureyev, and the Australian Ballet Company.

Sylvia

Any ballet with a score as consistently pleasing as Delibes', deserves to be seen – if only that it may be heard; but with Ashton's inventive choreography as well, (plus his steals from *La Source*, too) there is every reason to keep the eyes open. Add the Ironside brothers' wonderfully stylised Second Empire scenery and costumes, and there is still more reason to stay awake. Finally, add fine dancers with lots to occupy them: this all amounts to a good night out; yet, extraordinarily, the 1952 production embracing all these qualities, appears to be lost. In its full form, it made its last appearance in 1965; then, two years on, during the winter schedule, there was an attempt to show a cohesive one-act version – which failed. This was a bit like plucking some of the best stones from a tiara – and turning them into a brooch. Anyone who had seen the tiara, remembered its grand style; people who knew only the brooch, were not impressed by its lumpiness – somehow the *scheme* had vanished.

Ashton's role for Fonteyn had been a calculated exercise in broadening her 'attack' as a dancer; as the amazonian leader of Diana's band of huntresses, Sylvia in Act One was given expansive jumps (which had not been a Fonteyn forte) with a certain swagger of command. In Act Two, when Sylvia has been humanised by Eros' arrow, the dancer's poetic strengths were employed: Sylvia disconcerted by her vulnerability under capture. Act Three then added grandeur and bravado, particularly in Sylvia's fa-

Sylvia's dismay as she feels her strength ebb, with the first alien symptoms of love caused by Eros' arrow ... when moments before, she had mocked its power.

mous pizzicato solo. Fonteyn's method for driving herself through this particular display of fast footwork was to bet the conductor a magnum of champagne if he could get the orchestra to the last bar, before her. That was one cork he never heard pop.

Margot did just one performance in 1965; the jumping of Act One stressed an already inflamed knee, and although she hid the symptom, she was certain that the second billed performance would prove ruinous. In the event, she substituted *Swan Lake*. As she said, "Well, in a way, *that* one's easier. I just need to get up on point, and then I can *stay* there." Only Fonteyn could think that easier!

Having risked the wrath of Diana (previous page) by expressing her love for the mortal Aminta, Sylvia is eventually pardoned, and permitted to be united with him after he is restored by supernatural intervention from the effects of a more deadly arrow. In the wedding pas de deux, Fonteyn is here partnered by Attilio Labis.

as President, served the Academy tirelessly for the next 37 years. Very much a hands-on president, she not only organised star-studded fund-raising galas, over a number of years, but also found time to devise a new children's syllabus. I can recall her working over and over on this aspect, often on long-haul air flights when she might otherwise have been resting; but, as usual, once she had set her hand to it, she endlessly overhauled every detail. These pictures were taken during a visit to a putative new home for the academy, which plan also pre-occupied Margot. This base was set in the heart of Knightsbridge, in the old Llangattock town house (the name was the barony title of the head of the Rolls family) but the cost of re-building eventually got out of hand, and the site had to be abandoned to property speculators. It was a great tragedy that beneficiaries could not be found to secure the financial commitment, at the correct stage of this R.A.D. development plan, as the site must be gilt-edged, now.

I n the spring of 1954, Dame Adeline Genée announced her retirement from the presidency of the Royal Academy of Dancing, and of an instant, de Valois decided that Fonteyn would be the best replacement. She called Margot into her office and announced Dame Adeline's decision, then added, "It has been decided that you should replace Dame Adeline. You'll be taking over in July." Margot was nonplussed, and immediately countered, "But I don't *want* to be president of the Royal Academy of Dancing!" De Valois, ever the tactician, knew exactly when to click into her 'no opposition' mode: "Margot, I have a lot of other things to attend to, this morning, so if you don't mind, I'd like to get on with them, now." Margot, to her bafflement and annoyance, found herself once more in the corridor – and president-elect of the Academy! Of course, it proved to be a brilliant de Valois decision. Fonteyn,

Venice 1968, during appearances at La Fenice. The scene by the well was taken in the courtyard of the Ca' d' Oro, and I am uncertain if Margot knew that Taglioni once owned this mansion for a time, from 1847, when she was said to have made "ill-advised" alternations to the fabric. She also sold the beautiful well-head (which is by Bartolomeo Buono) to a dealer, and it was another fifty years before the house was restored by Baron Franchetti, who also managed to recover the well-head.

Hamlet

Robert Helpmann's 1942 one-act ballet is a canny distillate of the play's main elements, with a Freudian twist: the dying Hamlet is reliving the sequence in his mind, and in this nightmare span he can no longer sort out distinctly the characters of Ophelia and Gertrude. Leslie Hurry was the perfect designer for this approach; his asymmetrical costumes tease the mind; one knows something is 'off', but it is sometimes difficult to determine exactly what is prompting the feeling. His scenery is powerful, and 'dated' in the best sense – absolutely of its time, which was the London Blitz; it retains a very strong presence ... or did; one imagines scenery of this kind will never be properly restored, any more than the ballet itself.

Up to 1949, Fonteyn's appearances as Ophelia had amounted to 124 (Helpmann had done 159, as Hamlet) and then she did not return to the ballet again – except for two performances at the Baalbek Festival, fifteen years later. This was where I photographed it; and hereby hangs a strange matter. At the time of the 1964 London revival, for the Shakespeare Quatercentenary at Covent Garden, Margot was not included in the cast, which fact I found bitterly frustrating because, although I had never seen the ballet, the moment it was announced, I had the strongest mental picture of Margot, as a distraught

Ophelia, coming down a flight of stairs. It was so vivid, it was as if I had already taken the photograph. In the canteen one morning, Margot mentioned that she might still do the rôle, during the festival. I was excited by the prospect, and immediately explained the dramatic picture I planned to take, of Ophelia coming down the stairs. "There's only one problem," said Margot. "Ophelia's entrances don't use the stairs." This was very deflating news.

Due to all manner of intervening dramas, I had forgotten all about this sequence, by the time of the festival in Lebanon. At the rehearsal, Margot did indeed come on from the 'wings' on the lower level, that is, the flat stage area; but just before the performance, a big fake stone screen was unexpectedly moved by local technicians, quite blocking that part of the off-stage area. So, for her 'deranged' entrance, Margot had to improvise, from the o.p. side – and sure enough, down the long flight of real stone steps came the figure of Ophelia, wringing her hands, exactly as I had 'seen' and described, in the canteen in London. Afterwards, Margot was absolutely amazed. "You got your steps picture!" she said, with her eyes wide. The next night, we did some posed pictures, just to be certain; and that was the last time she wore that costume – for her 126th performance in the rôle.

Rudolf Nureyev as Hamlet.

Ian Hamilton as Laertes, and Henry Legerton as Polonius.

Ophelia's insanity.

By the time she had turned fifty, Margot's dancing calendar was probably fuller than it had ever been, with engagements all over the world, practically non-stop. Her age, for a ballerina, was not as remarkable as some people liked to suggest (Ulanova had been 49, at the time of her first, and only, London appearances) but nevertheless, Margot was genuinely surprised at the level of interest which persisted, and at the sometimes elaborate levels of persuasion which flowed from foreign managements. She was still deeply imbued with the idea that people should not be disappointed unnecessarily; and for every person who might have suggested that she was doing it 'for the money', the truth is that she could have taken administrative positions (not that the Royal Ballet ever offered one!) for less strain, and more recompense. Everyone knew that she had tremendous organisational capacities; that was a given. What some people failed to recognise was the fact that she was, heart and soul, a performing animal. 'The business' nurtured her. She was never dishonest about this. She listened to other people telling her what she ought to do; she knew backwards the mantras of going on too long; from her early thirties she had heard the lectures: that she was becoming remote; that she was headed for a middle-aged desert. Even in the matter of marriage, she was nagged at so often that she (unwisely) declared that she *would* marry, at 35 ... this, to silence the advisors' threnody. What really governed her, daily, was a deep, abiding interest in the problems of the stage, and an even more abiding interest in the problems of the studio, where one might – possibly – work out how such problems might best be overcome. Anyone who ignored this element of the Fonteyn persona was bound to be disconcerted, somewhere along the line.

After she was married, and in her newest rôle as Dutiful Wife, she parried further impertinent questions with the news that she would stop, instantly, if her husband asked her to. There was no danger of that scenario. She had married a foreign lawyer-politician whose interest in ballet extended principally to the capacities of the people who might be in the theatre box around him; there would be no point in snuffing out the *reason* why those people were in the box, in the first place; after all, they were there to see his wife! Of the countless people who had found Fonteyn's réclame engrossing, there were dancers who had gone through the company, treating Margot as a jolly – and often inspiring – colleague when, in truth, much of the publicity that had steered them to such a career, in the first instance, had been generated by the publicly-accounted exploits of the self-same colleague: Fonteyn! One such was John Cranko, who had headed to London from South Africa, straight after the war. By the early fifties, de Valois had recognised his interest in choreography, allowing him to create a piece for the young Svetlana Beriosova. She worked beautifully, but the ambitious young man was already dreaming of further conquests: a new piece for Fonteyn. His planning was smart enough to tap into the wealth of under-used Verdi ballet interludes, for a boulevard caprice to be known as *The Lady and the Fool*. In the event, de Valois vetoed his use of Fonteyn, but (as he once told me) "I went ahead, anyway. All that ballet was made as if Margot was going to dance The Lady."

By the end of the sixties, John Cranko was the acclaimed director and principal choreographer of a hugely talented young ballet company based in Stuttgart, and with all their success, he had never quite buried his wish to make something for Margot. He tried one more time, at the end of 1969 – and Margot said "yes" ... if he could fit it all into an appallingly tight spring schedule. John was elated. In the event, 'tight' would be an under-statement: something less than a week was available for rehearsals. The Stuttgart audiences, loyal to their own stars, were unimpressed by the news that Fonteyn would visit. As a jovial local said to me, "Ah! So this is your old ballerina?" I knew immediately that John, never mind Margot, had a steep slope ahead of him, but John was totally unfazed. After about the fourth day of rehearsals, he said to me one evening, with a shiver of glee, "I can't *wait* to see what she is going to do tomorrow!" It made me wonder if Margot was thinking the same thing about John. He had picked Scriabin's orgasmic score *The Poem of Ecstasy*, and the theme was to lean heavily on the perceived Fonteyn situation: ageing diva cannot surmount the brilliance of her past life; cue reflective withdrawal. Margot said not a word about this storyline.

Cranko's designer Jürgen Rose had skilfully married the whole concept to an evocation of the Jugendstil, in particular the mozaic complexities of Gustav Klimt's painted world. For a scene where the diva drifts asleep on a couch, and is possibly having a somewhat colourful dream about some of her past lovers, Rose devised a striking coup, with endless metres of painted parachute silk unfurling from the upper reaches, like some huge blot of coloured ink slowly enveloping an aquarium. This represented the lady's dream. The potential problem lay in the mechanics of the release; since there was so much silk on one beam, it developed its own inertia, en masse. However, once it descended, the effect was truly stunning. Margot was deeply conscious of the pressure under which Cranko worked. Even at the stage rehearsal they were still devising details. The actual ending had not been worked out. Cranko knew he wanted his diva alone on stage. "Margot! Just stay centre stage! Do something, until the curtain comes down. But don't move about!" Margot 'did' something, with her arms wreathing about her face. "Perfect," said John. Afterwards, Margot said, "I might be all right, if I can remember everything. If anything goes wrong, I've had it."

On the first night, all went well until the macguffin – the silk 'dream' – stuck tight! I was sitting in the director's box, which became tense with alarm at this point. On stage, Margot emoted a dream for what seemed like a long nightmare; then John erupted from his seat and rushed out of the box and along the rear corridor, shouting, "Bring the curtain down! Bring the curtain down!" It was a deeply shattering moment. The audience was fascinated. So this was the old ballerina! And she was merely lying still, on a couch! Perhaps she had collapsed?

I made my way, by degrees, backstage; and though I was mildly concerned as to the state of Margot's equilibrium, I was much more concerned about the state of the company's dancers; after all, this was a big night for them all, and one hated for their success to be compromised by ill luck. I needn't have worried about Margot. In order to take the boys' minds off events, she had immediately corralled them all, to act as princes in the Rose Adagio, which she proceeded to practice on the stage – with some tremendous balances. The boys were so engrossed in all this that I don't think the enormity of the situation had time to affect them. Finally, the stage management declared that they had solved the problem, and John went in front of curtain to announce that the ballet would begin again – "From the beginning!" Everything went swimmingly, next time around, and at the end, there was a sustained ovation. All thoughts about "old ballerinas" had been well and truly banished by Margot's remarkable physical allure in the part; the Stuttgarters were deeply impressed. In the matter of her star quality, before a potentially so-so foreign audience, it was deeply interesting to observe the Fonteyn 'pull'. Cranko had given her a very subtle, non-star, entrance: at a crowded salon full of guests undulating and gesticulating in conversation, the diva enters unannounced; her gloved hand emerging from behind the proscenium arch, to join other gloved hands; in fact, even when she emerges fully, she keeps her back to the audience until she reaches centre stage – and then a profile is glimpsed. In Stuttgart, at the first moment that particular hand appeared, the audience spontaneously burst into applause, and I am sure that most of them had no understanding of what had impelled them to do this, but it was electrifying to witness.

Poème de l'extase

With Egon Madsen as The Boy.

Richard Cragun as the image of a past love.

The Boy cannot compete with the glory of the diva's memories
– which, for her, have a haunting perfection eclipsing all
present reality.

*With leading men of the Stuttgart Ballet: Richard Cragun,
Heinz Clauss, Bernd Berg, Jan Stripling, and Egon Madsen.
A mathematics professor could write a long essay on the
harmonic exactitudes of Fonteyn's line at this instant.*

The diva's past sweeps her away from the present; with Richard Cragun and Egon Madsen.

In the garden of her mother's country address, with an overseas student. The statue represents Ondine mourning the dead Palemon.

Taking a curtain call at Covent Garden, after a performance of Frederick Ashton's Ondine, the ballet about the water nymph. Ashton had been a member of an Aegean boat cruise which included Fonteyn, and he had ample time to study Fonteyn's ease in the water.

Margot looking down into the Seine – and recalling the night when she was walking with Roland Petit in that vicinity, when Roland bet her she wouldn't dive in with him. Wrong move! Both dancers then shed their clothes and dived in. After swimming right across, and back again, they climbed out, got back into their clothes – and went to a nightclub!

With Rudolf Nureyev and Roland Petit, in London. At right: rehearsing Petit's ballet Paradise Lost.

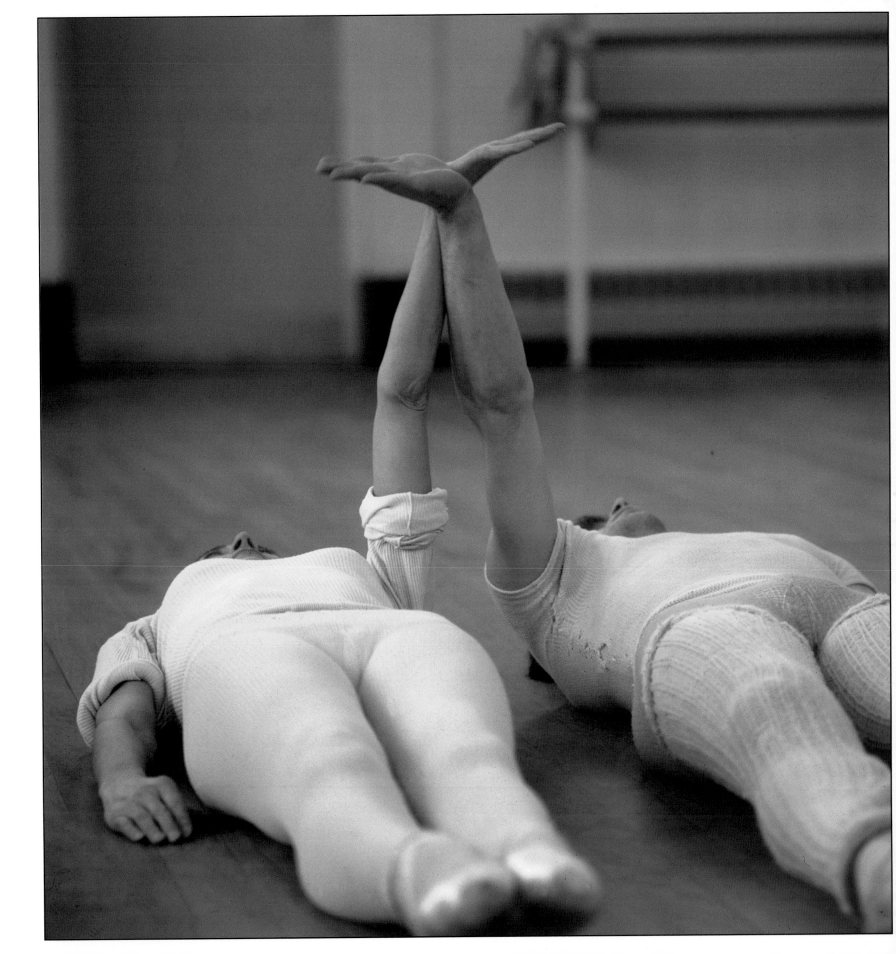

*Rehearsing Petit's second
ballet for Covent Garden,*
Pelléas et Melisande.

Performing La Sylphide *in Nice.*

Margot always had a tremendous rapport with children; here, she is with Cash Dewar, the son of Aubrey Dewar, who did much of the camerawork during our documentary.

The ballet pose comes from Ben Stevenson's version of Cinderella. *Taken during a performance for a television mixed bill, when Margot danced the pas de deux with Desmond Kelly.*

A rehearsal run-through for the Cinderella piece.

An extremely rare sight, this; Margot buying some flowers. She spent the greater part of her life being showered with expensive flowers at every turn, and if she sent flowers to other people, the accounts were usually mixed in with other items, later; so she was really quite shocked by the price of a small bunch of spring flowers on this particular day.

Walking from the opera house, Covent Garden, after a rehearsal in 1968.

Whether or not every picture tells a story, Margot's sombre expression in the Covent Garden street scene reminds me that she would have had plenty on her mind. It was a troubled period in her relationship with the Royal Ballet. Dancing is rightly seen as a rather insecure profession, and it is not unusual for younger members of a company to feel that they are perpetually singled out for managerial slights and oversights; that somehow their true worth is not being recognised. If it is any comfort, managerial slights can attend the greatest. Fonteyn, for many years (24 in this instance,) was the archetypal rep dancer within the company, never behaving as if she was greater than it, and serving it faithfully and continually, not least at times when she was offered handsome lures to move elsewhere; and she was willing always to stand in for colleagues at short notice, if asked. Hers was not star behaviour, even though the box office held evidence that she was a very big star indeed. De Valois had put her faith in Miss Hookham at an early stage of her development, and thereafter, Miss Hookham repaid that trust a thousandfold.

And then, one day in the summer of 1959, the administrative board at Covent Garden damaged that trust with a piece of high-handed and cynical opportunism such as often attends powerful bodies used to creating their own laws; they raised the seat prices for any performance in which Fonteyn appeared. It never crossed the corporate mind that the dancer in question should be informed, let alone consulted.

It was only when a banner label across a new programming poster, on the wall of the opera house, caught Margot's eye, that she learned of the plan. She was outraged by the scheme, most particularly because she sensed immediately that it would penalise the very people who had supported the Sadler's Wells Ballet with great loyalty, during the difficult war years and beyond: ordinary people with ordinary wages; theirs was the support which had helped to burnish the company's prestige. Why should they be penalised, by the appearance of one dancer? Margot went straight to the General Administrator's office. David Webster was sitting behind his desk, in his habitual pose: one leg cocked over the other, as he idly scratched under a sock at an irritating skin condition. He continued this activity, while listening to Margot's complaint, which she wound up by saying, "This is the sort of thing they do for guest artists, and I'm *not* a guest artist." Her implication was that the latter were of a breed with which she felt no affinity, whatsoever. Webster was smoothly non-commital. "Well, dear, I'll consider all that you've said." He then ceased the scratching; the interview was clearly at an end.

Two weeks later, Margot returned from a brief trip to Rio de Janeiro, and in the taxi from the airport she opened that morning's *Times* and at some point glanced at the social column, where she was astounded to notice that, "Dame Margot Fonteyn has become a Guest Artist with the Royal Ballet Company." Elsewhere, in an interview, David Webster parried suggestions that the situation was unusual: "This arrangement has been made at the suggestion of the company and with the agreement of Dame Margot." The latter statement was fanciful, and Webster had plainly taken a calculated gamble; "The Liverpool Draper" (a nickname earned from an earlier calling) had a reputation for cutting his cloth at unlikely angles, if he could spot an advantage. Margot could either accept the situation, or dance elsewhere – deprived of many of her best ballets. So much for the state of play at the opera house. At the Ballet School, the rest of the company assumed, quite naturally, that Margot had asked for more money, and that she had been accommodated. The general view could be paraphrased as, "It's reasonable. After all, she has only got a year or two left, and our wages have *always* been lousy." De Valois, juggling the needs of her company within that of the greater empire of the opera house, managed to smooth this disquiet with her own brand of counsel, and life went on much as before. When, four years on, de Valois relinquished the day-to-day running of the company, it was a watershed in more than one respect. She had achieved all her main goals for her creation: the company was nationally endorsed, with a Royal Charter; it had international status; it was financially viable; it had developed exceptional performing talent in depth; and even in choreographic matters – that most elusive of talents – there was already in place a logical heir to Ashton. Thus, the company could paddle boldly, without any need to touch the bottom of the pool.

One year on, and a sea-change had crept through the company's headquarters. Increasingly, Fonteyn was being made to feel she was *de trop*. There was no honest, open-handed discussion about policy, merely a mean-spirited, veiled form of 'making life difficult', which (I can attest) reduced even Margot to tears – once she was safely out of the building. Although it is hard to credit, Assistant Director Hart actually said to me, in November 1964, in relation to Fonteyn: "That woman is *nothing* to do with this company." The statement was so bizarre, that I responded with, 'But for that woman, you would not be in a position to stand here and tell me that." This remark promptly got me banned from the Royal Ballet School, and banned from backstage at the Opera House too – until lawyers decided otherwise.

What was the reality behind this feverish situation? Historically, it has always presented problems, when a ballet company and an opera company are both governed by the same board, and it would need a fourteen day week to satisfy everyone. At Covent Garden, in the early days of the Ashton regime at the Royal Ballet, a rough average of the performances allocated to ballet was 3.5 per week. Seen from the ballet buildings, this was restrictive; seen from Covent Garden, where financial considerations stalked the corridors, there was always concern that ticket sales could be squeezed consistently past 85%, if there were more than three performances a week, of ballet. The Received Story, of this mid sixties period in the Royal Ballet's history, is that the continuing presence of Fonteyn in the programmes was, *apparently*, a barrier to the progression of the other ballerinas. From the theatre management's point of view, Fonteyn's name and presence allowed them a comforting forward projection; they knew the house returns for those nights on which she would dance, from the moment they pencilled in her name. Still, let us now study the ballerinas' cries; let us close in on the autumn of 1964, when this groundswell gained currency. In this period, Fonteyn was not in evidence in either the first, or second, week. In the third week, she was not in a triple bill either; she and Nureyev were listed for 1 *Giselle*; and Page and Gable were listed for 1 *Coppélia*. In the event, Page could not do her *Coppélia*, which caused Lane and Usher to step in; and, coincidentally, Park did not appear in the Peasant pas de deux in *Giselle*. Fourth week: Lane did her scheduled *Coppélia*; there was a triple bill involving numerous ballerinas – none of whom was Fonteyn; and then there were two performances of *Giselle*: one with Nerina and Blair (with Park absent again) and one with Fonteyn and Nureyev (in which the absentee, this time, was Sibley). Fifth week: it was the turn of Beriosova and MacLeary, in *Giselle*. MacLeary couldn't go on, and was replaced by Blair. Fonteyn and Nureyev did their *Swan Lake* (in which both Park, and Sibley, were absent in Act Three) and Nerina and Blair did their *Swan Lake* (in which both Park and Sibley were absent again). Thus closed Week Five, in which the three senior ballerinas had each done one full-length ballet. Came Week Six, in which the paying public

and the box office management were jointly wondering just how many times a representative was going to be sent out front, to announce a cast change. For this week, and Week Seven, there was only one sold out night (guess who); this left 7 more *Swan Lakes* to be negotiated by senior dancers. Would they make it? MacLeary couldn't go on with Beriosova, and was then replaced by Gable; Page couldn't go on with Blair, and both had to be replaced by Beriosova and Gable; Sibley couldn't go on, with Gable, and had to be replaced by Seymour; Nerina then had to replace Seymour, the following week ... and so on, in bewildering medley. Of the ballerinas with two functioning legs under them, Fonteyn did 2 *Giselles* and 2 *Swan Lakes*; Nerina did 1 *Giselle* and 3 *Swan Lakes*; Beriosova did 1 *Giselle* and 3 *Swan Lakes*; and of the men, Gable did 1 *Swan Lake* with Nerina, 2 with Beriosova, and 1 with Seymour, and in the entire season, he would partner nine of the company's ballerinas – Fonteyn included! When *The Sleeping Beauty* went into the repertory, over Christmas, Fonteyn did 3 performances with Blair (spread over five weeks); Page and Sibley both dropped out; Nerina did 2; Beriosova did 2; Park did 2; and Nerina also did *La fille mal gardée*. Park, at this point, so disliked the idea of having to dance Aurora that she declared she would only go on if she wasn't required to rehearse. All this is now viewed, historically, as an untenable situation, with Fonteyn squeezing out the other dancers! The Covent Garden administration probably heard none of this, yet its box office might well have had a different slant, on exactly how oppressive it really was: to have Fonteyn still dancing, when asked, at Covent Garden. Complaints about Fonteyn 'taking performances' sometimes came from ballerinas who could not consistently fulfil the performances they had been allocated; there seemed to be festering a notion (not discounted by the administrative office) that, if *only* Fonteyn would stay in some *other* country, then deserving heads would receive the spotlight more often, get cheered more often, and written about favourably, more often. If only ...

There is very little that can be said about the early days of the MacMillan version of *Romeo and Juliet*, that has not already been recounted, by everyone, on every hand – myself included. We know the Hurok Organisation pressured Covent Garden, by insisting that Fonteyn do the première; I have recounted Margot's own efforts to persuade Hurok to launch the ballet in New York with Gable and Seymour as the star-cross'd pair; of Fonteyn's Juliet, Lady MacMillan is keen to emphasise, more than thirty years on, that "Kenneth never really liked her in the rôle," and so on. (Lady MacMillan might add – and perhaps does – that Kenneth never much liked Rudolf in *his* rôle, either.) With all this bitter recrimination *still* circulating, newcomers could be forgiven for thinking that this ballet's première had been a calamity; but 43 curtain calls do not attend disasters. Ashton's strong pragmatic streak, concerning the 'hows' of theatrical management, had, at a crucial moment, come down on the side of the im-

presario, so Margot's championing of the younger pair was wasted. When she did catch up with events (she was never really told *anything*) she was disconcerted: that her choreographic mentor was on the one hand making life difficult in respect of his own ballets, while loading her onto someone else's. She knew she was being used purely as a safety net for a financial enterprise, and she felt desperately unsupported in what was, by any reckoning, an enormous challenge – for *any* dancer. Launching a three act ballet in which she had barely received the framework of the steps, she was also expected to cope with insidious layers of pressure, yet still pull the rabbit out of the hat, on the vital night, for MacMillan. Of *course* Kenneth had a rough deal, having his chosen dancers usurped. Of *course* it was traumatic for the dancers concerned (amongst whom I would mention Fonteyn; just imagine *those* pressures!) Of course... But, at the end of the day, Theatre has its dramas on stage *and* off, and it always will; and it is extraordinary that this matter of casting precedence in February 1965 was, it seems, allowed to poison entire careers, thereafter. At the time, it was a matter of eight days, until the Seymour/Gable début, when anyone with the slightest interest in the matter had the chance to decide how much the *ballet* had suffered, by being launched with a double-starred pair. Seymour and Gable were wonderful in their rôles; but, in quite different ways, so were Fonteyn and Nureyev; and everyone was in agreement: that MacMillan had provided wonderful opportunities for all of them. The ballet itself lives on.

Romeo and Juliet

The nurse (Gerd Larsen) intimates to Juliet that her new maturity will bring her to the attention of prospective suitors, amongst whom is her father's front-runner, the noble and handsome Paris (Derek Rencher) who is soon enough given an opportunity to admire the daughter of the House of Capulet, at a lavish Capulet ball.

Also at the ball, and temporarily disguised (due to a lack of the proper invitations) is Romeo (Rudolf Nureyev) with his two closest friends, Mercutio (David Blair) and Benvolio (Anthony Dowell). As a member of the Montagu clan, factionally opposed to the Capulets, in the power-play politics of Verona, Romeo is viewed as an undesirable within Capulet walls, particularly by the hot-head Capulet cousin, Tybalt (Desmond Doyle).

On the ballroom floor, Romeo is suddenly transfixed by the sight of Juliet; at first, he is scarcely aware that she is of the household; he is concerned only with gaining her attention. In this endeavour, he is aided and abetted by light-hearted musical accompaniment from his friends in the background. During a supper interval, Juliet conspires to evade the attentions of her nurse, and meets up with the young man from the ballroom ...

... and as soon as he discards his mask, a mutual attraction is set fully alight. When Tybalt interrupts this innocent tryst, Romeo is caught without his disguise, and a sequence of half-hearted subterfuge is soon enough brought to an end by Tybalt, who orders Romeo to leave. An unseemly fracas is only avoided by the intervention of Lord Capulet, who declares that the code of hospitality must prevail.

Below, the pivotal conjunction in which the fate of all three is sealed. While Romeo beats a pragmatic retreat (the better to effect a return) the attentions of both Tybalt and Juliet are irrevocably focussed on a single target: the one from mounting hatred, the other from new-found infatuation.

Later that same night, a further tryst – below Juliet's bedroom balcony – leads to rapturous entanglements and expressions of devotion. As Juliet has already decided that the noble Paris is also a noble bore, the mad-cap device of a secret marriage to the dashingly exciting Romeo is – with the conspiracy of a devoted nurse – arrived at; and in the chapel of Father Lawrence, the pair are joined by the vows of matrimony.

Back in the family mansion once more; after a single night with Romeo, Juliet finds the realities of home life swirling about her: Lord Capulet is determined that she shall accept Paris' suit in marriage. She is even displayed in her own bedroom, like an heirloom under barter. Lady Capulet ignores her daughter's pleas for moral support, while Paris is urged to take a stronger line; he then conducts the girl forcefully in a few measures of a courtly dance. Juliet, emotionally drained, reacts more as a puppet – until she summons the strength to reject Paris physically. At this, her irate and implacable father leaves her to ponder upon her rebelliousness. She shall *marry* this 'suitable' suitor.

Desperate stakes – desperate measures. Juliet flees to Friar Lawrence for help, whereupon this ecclesiastical 'flake' produces the sort of remedy which can only go wrong, even on a good day. Juliet must drink a frightful potion which will render her 'as dead' ... until she is safely out of sight in the family tomb. There, the banished Romeo will hasten, to effect rescue. Thus speaks the friar.

Of course, Romeo does not get the proper message, and tragedy ensues. If there remains a true and timeless message in all this, it must be: never trust a messenger service; and never, ever, ask men wearing long brown dresses, for advice.

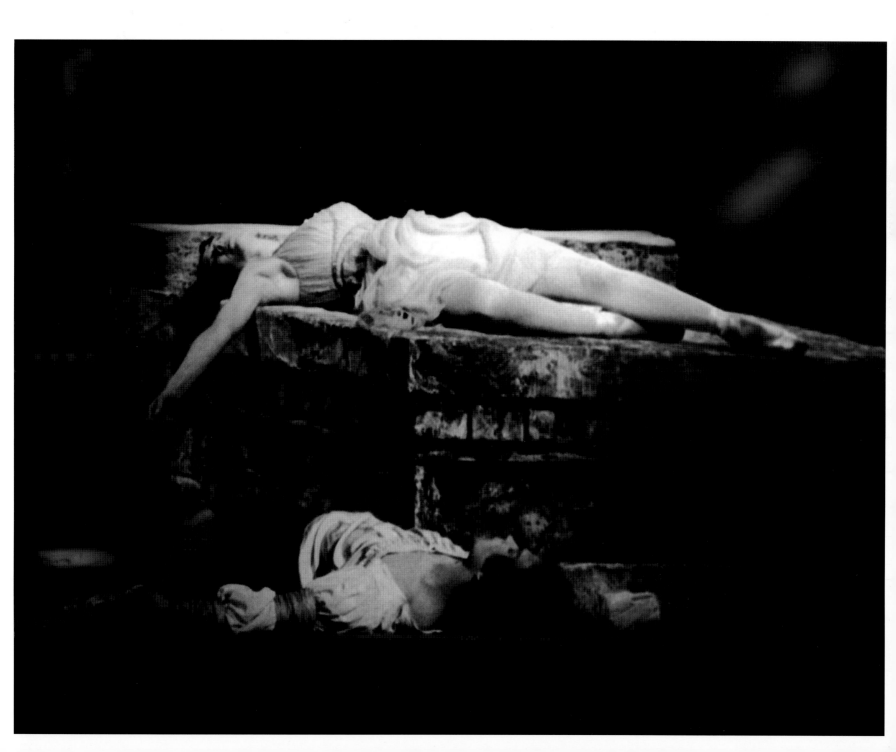

Taken at one of the rehearsals for the new production of Romeo and Juliet, *before the pressure of events knocked the smile off every face ...*

A year before all the dramas surrounding R & J, Kenneth MacMillan had made an interesting piece for Fonteyn and Nureyev, for the Bath Festival. It used a Bartok violin piece, with no less than Menuhin playing the accompaniment. Both dancers adjusted very happily to MacMillan's idiom, and it was unfortunate chance that this abstract work was never seen by a wider audience.

Divertimento

Photographed during the performance at the Presidential Inaugural Gala in Washington, 1965. Margot improvised her curtain call stance, to take account of the huge audience in the raked Armory seats high above her.

Le Corsaire

After the performance, and the arrival of gallant South American admirers who have not been told that ballerinas, and stairs, can co-exist.

Fonteyn and Nureyev and traffic congestion, during a stage rehearsal; and backstage before the performance, with Joan Thring standing in as dresser.

In 1968, having retired Messel's glorious production of The Sleeping Beauty, the Royal Ballet launched a new production – with many changes, including a Mediaeval setting. Lila di Nobili's costume for Aurora had a skirt of extremely dubious lineage which really did nothing for the choreography, or any ballerina executing it. Di Nobili had done well for Margot, with her Ondine dress, but her Aurora 'frock' earned no plaudits. Margot could hardly believe it, and mocked the poor garment endlessly. "How could they possibly expect a dancer to wear this?!" As she built up a hatred for the dress, so her catalogue of 'alternative uses' for the thing grew also. At one point, she ran through a swift sequence of cameos, improvising themes; one was an Edwardian girl going to her first adult party; another was a haughty girl at the Paris Lido, over-dressed on top, and clearly under-dressed, below. The costume was a shocker; it always had the appearance of having been in the rain, as well as a profile which suggested Aurora had hidden a birthday picnic to the rear. It annoyed Margot so much that, for a while, she took herself out of the work altogether. In the end, she relented for a U.S. tour, but her wariness about that production remained on high alert.

Margot was someone for whom the business of class and rehearsal held abiding interest. She never tired of the routine, because she felt that it wasn't a routine; each day held a fresh set of problems, and some of these required fresh solutions. Her concentration was absolute. To watch her during pauses in a class was to sense a computer humming away. All her awareness was engaged in that room, in that hour; all other problems were 'on hold'. She would be listening, assessing, studying others ... almost impatient for the next sequence. In rehearsals, as she studied her own line in the mirror, I sometimes wondered who it was she saw there, because there was no 'collusion', between the self, and the mirrored self: her appraisal was detached in the way of someone comparing bolts of cloth, or wallpaper. Not this; not that; possibly; perhaps a shade darker; no – the one with smaller dots was better; but on the other hand, that one, with *this* one ... and one knew that, at another level, these comparisons were still continuing, even as fresh configurations began to replace the earlier set.

This intensity of application – the ordered and indexed mind – was ratcheted up several notches once a performance was due; but at that point something else occurred: she could park that first level somewhere (humming away!) whilst wheeling in the 'performance day trolley': the practical, jolly, un-phased, alert-to-everyone-else, Margot the Trouper trolley. I have seen her, well within the half-hour of a big night, dealing with someone else's problem headdress; quelling someone else's nerves; telling funny stories; even steering a colleague through a drink-aggravated, full-on nervous breakdown.

Once the wings were reached, the day *really* began. It was like a good horse, just before a race: the energy contained, yet already moving towards an objective. In *Beauty*, her warming-up even included her face, which was required to carry that 16-year-old princess's *joie-de-vivre*. In the wings area once, just before the Birthday act, I heard a weird noise, behind a scenery flat, sounding like a trapped bird: the beating of wings in high tempo; but it turned out to be coming from Margot, at the rosin box. She was working her lips and tongue and eyelids and cheek muscles in frighteningly noisy full revs; then, by degrees, all this was wound back, until it was ticking imperceptibly – just like a Rolls-Royce engine.

In Panama, during a rare break in her performing schedule. Margot was always entirely happy if the sea was in earshot. These pictures were taken with a miniature spy camera – which just shows the sort of quality that spy masters will put up with.

Early in her public life, Margot learned that it was unwise to admit to a favourite this or that, for it would always be quoted back at her, endlessly, until whatever it was became distinctly un-favourite. However, in the matter of ballets, she did have a favourite, and it was *Daphnis and Chloë*, which she simply adored performing – and she performed it simply, and quite perfectly. It is true that she liked *Ondine*, very much – although the shadow dance irritated her no end – but Chloë was 'home', for her. For this one, she tapped some well-spring of joy and commitment concerning basic matters to do with love's attractions, the power of the sun, and, most importantly, the compulsion to dance in daily life. And with one of the world's great orchestral scores to dance to, one can hardly doubt that she meant it, at the deepest level, when she said that, in *Daphnis*, "everything just happens." No-one who saw her in this work could forget the timeless gravitas of her dance to the flute solo; certainly, from the moment I first saw it, I knew that Ballet, at its best, could be profoundly satisfying. This 1951 Ashton ballet had a struggle at the start; amongst various reservations there had been a reprise of the 1912 argument: that Ravel's score was too perfect to admit illustration. By the early sixties, a perfect Chloë was lacking a perfect Daphnis. No easy matter, this; one could make a long list of why some things do and do not work for the dancer who has to take this rôle, and there is little that the dancer can do about it. When Margot discovered my feelings about this ballet, she was quite prepared to discuss it in detail, on the basis of a parity of passion about the subject. She was clear that the ballet had not been working, and that casting concerned her – to the point where she wondered if she would dance it again. This seemed a desperate prognosis. I was certain I knew who would be a perfect Daphnis; I knew too that it would be pointless to come straight out with this, and there was quite a long period when I floated extremely oblique hints; indeed, so oblique, that I was sure they had drifted past their target by several miles. Then, one day, à propos of nothing to do with that day's events, Margot suddenly said, "You're right, you know." At that moment, I knew she was talking about Christopher Gable being Daphnis – so I was careful to say nothing at all in response, and left this seed floating on the surface of the pond. (Early on, Margot had made it clear she didn't see Rudolf in the rôle.) But I knew that this was where the troubles really began, for Margot had entered that bleak period in her relationship with the Royal Ballet, wherein the management with ill-grace occasionally pencilled her into the big classics, to appease the box office, while slicing away the majority of the Ashton works which really sustained her own interest in the London repertory. My own view was that she should fight back; that if she was helping to carry the big classics, then they owed her one. (I had also conceived an ambition to film *Daphnis and Chloë*, and was delighted to find that Margot, despite her huge reservations about that medium, was happy to contemplate this scheme.) "But they'll never let us do it," she said, with a knowledge of the factors ranged against her, that I barely guessed at that stage. By degrees, I urged her on, arguing that she had to do something that was rewarding to her, if she was to sustain all the other. When finally I discussed the notion with Christopher, a fresh problem arose; it hadn't crossed my mind that he would be entirely unimpressed with the addition of Fonteyn's name to the nine or ten other ballerinas he was expected to partner at this period. What I *could* foresee was the ballet management saying, "Oh God, she's bored with Nureyev; now she's going to pinch this one!" *Tant pis.* I was determined this thing would happen, and thank goodness Margot was steadily warming to the challenge. Finally, I judged that she was strong enough to confront the main barrier, and so gave her a metaphorical shove. Next day, back came the answer: "They won't let me. They say it's out of the question." "You didn't put your case strongly enough." "You weren't there." I gave her another shove: "Confront Fred directly; don't let yourself be mauled by Michael and Jack, like a rag doll." She shook her head. "You don't know what it's like." "There are some things I *do* know, and this is one of them." So, off she went. Late in the afternoon, she came back. She looked very tired – but calm, in an interesting way. "Oh – it was so awful. I said to Fred, quite simply, that I wanted to do *Daphnis*, and I wanted to do it with Christopher, and I didn't want to have to fight over it. Fred was absolutely *furious*. Finally he shouted, 'Oh, very well. *Do whatever you want to!*' and then walked out of the office!" This was all a bit much to take in, but in the final analy-

sis, I felt sure that Ballet itself would be the winner, which seemed to justify all the stupid anguish. Of course, they got their own back. Margot was right: we were never allowed to film the production. But I still have an 1890 limited edition of the Elizabethan version of Amyot's translation from the only existing copy of the Longus classic. In it is an inscription: "For Keith – may your dream come true," and it is signed "Chloë". Dreams are strange things. And anyway, in England, and Europe, and America, over the following two years, all sorts of new audiences discovered *Daphnis and Chloë*, and perhaps some of them still remember it, with Fonteyn and Gable.

Rehearsing, with Christopher Gable as Daphnis.

Daphnis and Chloë

Chloë shapes:
her solo to the flute, in which she celebrates safe passage from
harm, through means of archaic, ritual gestures and accents;
and her hard-angled, resistant imagery, when she becomes
entangled with Dorkon, the village 'loud boy', (Ronald Hynd).

Fonteyn and Gable against John Craxton's décor.

179

The dance competition is won by Daphnis.

Abraxas the pirate chief (Alexander Grant) raids the village at night, and Chloë is abducted and taken to a coastal lair. Terrified and helpless, with her wrists bound, the captive is bullied and taunted by the chief. Meanwhile, the villagers have sought intercession by the muses of Pan's Grotto, and at dawn, the god himself intercedes. Daphnis, having searched for Chloë all night, has collapsed by the seashore, exhausted. As day breaks, Pan deposits Chloë, unharmed, on the shore, where Daphnis is lying ...

The reunion of the goatherd and the shepherdess signals, for the village, an excuse for a Betrothal celebration, and there, Chloë eventually arrives dressed in new finery (one imagines a grandmother tenderly removing this outfit from a family chest) and the story is concluded with exultant flourishes of joy from the village's teenage pack.

Daphnis and Chloë reunited at dawn, by the sea's edge.

Chloë's arrival in the final scene of Daphnis and Chloë – *a picture taken during a remarkable evening in the history of English theatre, when the Royal Ballet mounted a tribute to Sir Frederick Ashton, in 1970, at the time of his retirement. This latter situation was yet another coup promoted by Sir David Webster of the opera house. With the full knowledge of de Valois (whose brand of forward thinking had already raced on, to Phase Three of her Plan for Continuity) Webster did not offer Ashton the choice of extending his original 7-year contract, despite his having helmed the greatest theatrical advancement in the company's post-war history.*
The entire company managed to keep secret from the director its complex planning for this panoramic revue of his remarkable career, which contained 36 different extracts – many reconstructed from ballets considered to be lost or forgotten. It was a matter of relentless archeology, far and wide, and the secret was maintained right to the rise of the curtain; even the programmes were only given out after the event. As a theatrical evening, it was the coup des coups.

The traditional image of theatre people, as gypsies of no fixed abode, has receded – due to television knocking out many forms of repertory theatre and the ever-spiralling costs of big-company tours. However, in the 20th century, until the end of the seventies, this code of necessary impermanence still prevailed, and theatre people strove to establish 'fixed abodes' in the face of shifting jobs, or lack thereof; and if a home *was* fixed, it often lay empty. In Margot's case, she was really the archetypal theatrical gypsy. From the age of eight, from the moment her parents took her on that first momentous trip to America and China, she began to absorb an alternative lifestyle to that of traditional home life (in the European sense at least) which saw 'home' as a fixed and localised base, to which a family became bound by a pattern of continuity. Due to her father's internment in Shanghai throughout the war years, and then the subsequent mutually agreed ending of her parents' marriage, Margot's base devolved upon her mother's (English) base, wherever it might be. By war's end, her brother had launched himself into a career (inevitably photography) – and also marriage. Margot felt responsible for her mother's situation; she understood the sacrifices that had been made, and also their corollary: that Mrs Hookham, to a degree, now lived through her daughter's career. This might have produced its own pressures, yet each was wonderfully adjusted to the other's presence. In *her* role, as the 'theatrical mum', Mrs Hookham displayed the greatest tact – not least in keeping a tight rein on overt expressions of pride in her daughter's advancement. But equally, she did not want to feel she was somehow living in her daughter's house – so it was always a finely-tuned balancing act. When Margot finally married, it was to someone who abandoned a young family, and a fixed base; and a sense of impermanence still prevailed, due to a husband's political aspirations, and his maverick tendency to shift bases accordingly. Margot could be wistful about her friends' homes – and in many of these, her own possessions were quartered in odd corners, as overflow from her mother's packed cupboards. She was not good at throwing things away, and as her fame grew, so people increasingly thrust gifts towards her, and then these too required cupboards. There was always a hunt for hidden corners: for some years, the big Annigoni portrait hung in *my* London sitting room, because *my* ceilings happened to be high enough; other friends maintained racks of her Paris clothes; still others kept cases of her French wine in their cellars. And all the while, Margot, I know, had this sweet dream about retiring, and gathering all these things together, and sitting at the centre of a *real home*. It never quite happened. When she did retire, and went to live in Panama, the circumstances had altered, the climate was different, and the imperative for being surrounded by the trappings of a successful life had faded. So, all her 'bits and pieces' just slumbered on, elsewhere. Yet, in one way, she had really worked it perfectly: for the stage had *truly* been her home – and there was really nothing that could compete with the endless richness of all that.

Margot in the hotel suite which became her only home, for several years.

Marguerite and Armand

If you had stood outside the foyer of the opera house at Covent Garden, on the night of 12th March 1963, button-holing patrons as they emerged into the cool night air after the hot-house fevers of this one act ballet; and if you had said to them, "In ten years time, people will still be streaming out into this street, after seeing this ballet, with exactly this cast, producing exactly this hubbub of chatter," then you would have been told you were either insane or drunk; and if you had persisted in this crazed pre-

diction, it is possible that you might have been picked up by both elbows and then deposited in the foyer of the Bow Street police station, immediately opposite, where they would have advised some fresh air and a good night's rest. Well, Mr Ripley, the rest is history ... Sir Frederick Ashton's cunning 'vehicle' just kept rollin' along, and Fonteyn's faltering exit, after the scene of the insult with the banknotes, became one of the iconographic theatre images of the age, with audiences audibly moved. *Quelle artiste*!

Marguerite, the lady of the camellias and the belle of the salons ...

Everything about this ballet was somehow larger than life, including the fact that it got filmed *twice*, thirteen years apart! (Alas, the first was too mucked about, and the other was too late.) Nureyev's greatest, most histrionic, performance may have been that of the full dress rehearsal, when he took off his Beaton-designed jacket at one point, and with extraordinary passion, tore it into several quite small pieces. One could even suggest that the nonconformist Sixties actually began that morning, beyond the stage-bay doors of Floral Street, to the sound of that ripping clothing – just after these photographs were taken. If *Time* had been sharper, it could have been called "Ripping London", which would have been more correct vernacular English than the subsequent "Swinging" label they applied. It is ironic, in the light of subsequent events, that Ashton actually listed a second cast when this ballet was first launched: his choices were Seymour and Gable.

With the excitement provoked by the hot-house attentions of the salon's somewhat raw new recruit, Marguerite's incipient illness suddenly produces a bout of feverish coughing. Half fainting, she subsides onto a chaise, to recover her composure. There is mild concern in the room, from those who know that Marguerite's health is uncertain. Armand knows none of this, seeing the move only as some ploy to gain his attention further. He sweeps onto the chaise, to express, with elaborate civility, his concern. Marguerite struggles to regain her composure; already her interest has been kindled ...

In the crowded salon, Marguerite casts down one of the camellias she has been wearing, as a sign that it may be retrieved by someone attentive ... and Armand forcefully commands others to step aside, so that he may retrieve the bloom himself. Marguerite admires his youthful authority.

An idyll in the country with Armand is too wonderful to last. The arrival of Armand's father (Michael Somes) pleading that the association will ruin his son's future prospects, leads Marguerite to the bitter conclusion that she must sever the relationship.

203

In the country retreat, Marguerite attempts to hide her distress from Armand, and to suggest that nothing is amiss ...

Marguerite's public humiliation by Armand (who has hurled a fistful of banknotes at her) leaves a broken woman. Too late, Armand Père betrays some recognition of the sacrifice she has made, for his son.

Cinderella

Ashton's first full-length ballet, for the Sadler's Wells company's new home at the opera house, was a calculated plan to trap a random audience over the Christmas season; the potential extra ingredient being countless children on the loose, with equal numbers of distracted parents. For this mission, *Cinderella* was the perfect alternative to *The Sleeping Beauty*. Outside Russia there was no example of a home-grown, contemporary, full-length ballet; but with so many resources under one roof, this was the company best suited to trying such a thing in 1948. Besides which, Prokofiev's score was then available; half the problem was already solved. The *travesti* element of this Ashton production has come to be seen as a homage to British music hall tradition, though it was originally planned for the ugly sisters to follow the Russian mode: played by girls. When Moyra Fraser absented herself from the company at a crucial point in the rehearsals, Ashton then pulled Margaret Dale aside and took over *her* rôle as the

timid sister, with Robert Helpmann rampaging in Fraser's place. Both enjoyed themselves so much that there was never going to be a chance for the girls to reclaim their places. There were other changes: Fonteyn tore a ligament, a month before the première, and was replaced by the alternate casting of Moira Shearer. There still seems to be an echo of both dancers in the choreography for the heroine: the light, quick variations in the kitchen suggest Shearer's hallmark, while the big pas de deux in the ballroom is so replete with variations on the arabesque, that it is surely Ashton's homage to Fonteyn's capacity. In this pas de deux, she somehow increased the pressure by degrees, so that the content grew dynamically to a climax somewhere within the span; and then she wound it all in again until, at the end, it was like some craft coming to rest in a harbour, with all sails beautifully furled. As for the way she could stop, magically frozen in mid turn, on the first 'clock chime' ... this always seemed quite uncanny.

Left alone in the gloomy old kitchen, Cinderella dresses her broom as a dancing partner ...

Cinderella is made tearful by the unkindness of her two belligerent step-sisters, and by thoughts of the happy times when her mother was still alive. Her father (Leslie Edwards) attempts to comfort her, but soon enough retreats from the carry-on of his frightful step-daughters. When they attempt to drive off an old beggar woman seeking alms, Cinderella intervenes, giving the old woman the bread she had put aside for her own humble meal. At this, one of the sisters is about to slap Cinderella for her act of defiance when, of an instant, a strange light fills the kitchen, making the step-sister (Frederick Ashton) fearful. By contrast, Cinderella senses something strangely powerful has entered their domain ... and of course, it turns out that the old woman is none other than the Fairy Godmother in disguise, and with her magical intervention, Cinderella is thus enabled to attend the Prince's Ball, which had seemed to be denied her earlier by her unkind sisters' edict. Eventually, she arrives in the royal ballroom (next pages) escorted by an entourage of godmotherly fairies and pages. She enters in a trance, overcome by the wonder of her situation.

Cinderella, alone in the ballroom during a supper entertainment, has a moment to express her own excitement and wonder at events ...

Cinderella and the prince: the grand ballroom pas de deux –
an essay on the arabesque. David Blair as the prince.

The fairy godmother's attendants form a protective cordon around the prince and Cinderella.

As a signal of his approval, the prince bestows on Cinderella a tray of three rare and costly oranges. Emboldened by the fact that her step-sisters have still failed to recognise her in her unfamiliar finery, Cinderella gives two of the oranges to them. Soon enough, the more forceful of the two (Robert Helpmann) manages to trick the other into surrendering the largest orange, and in the small hours of the morning, when she is back by the family hearth recounting the wonders of the ball (right) she produces this orange, to score a point over her less forceful sister (Frederick Ashton). But Cinderella is hiding her own keepsake from a wonderful and bewildering evening: for when she failed to remember the fairy godmother's warning, about leaving the ball before the stroke of midnight – and so had to flee the castle, just as her finery was transformed back into her dull costume – she lost one of the exquisite slippers; but the other somehow stayed with her. Finding this slipper tucked into her apron, later, she realises that the whole episode cannot have been a mere dream.

After a tireless quest to find, somewhere in the prince's kingdom, the girl whose foot exactly fits the glass slipper, the royal search party arrives at the house of Cinderella's father. When the step-sisters fail to force their own gross feet into the delicate shoe, Cinderella is given a chance. As soon as she has placed the slipper neatly on her foot, for good measure she produces the other slipper from the pocket of her apron, and fits that one, too. There is an eruption of joy, amazement, and step-sisterly dismay, as the prince kneels to take the hand of the girl he has been seeking ever since the night of the ball. Later, in a magical apotheosis, he leads Cinderella towards a bright new life.

223

Ondine's first entrance, through the waterfall.

Ondine

Frederick Ashton's fourth three-act ballet had a very protracted gestation period; he had become very interested in the subject after admiring Jean Giraudoux's play, which he had seen in Paris in 1939. His eventual homage to his prima ballerina picked up on Fonteyn's strong affinity with water; and the tale of the water sprite, who traps a mortal, had an undertow of Gothic acidity which exactly suited the 'shadow side' of Ashton, which positively warmed to elements of melancholy and blighted passion. (Margot once remarked, "I think Fred's absolutely *perfect* day would *have* to include something that wasn't *quite* perfect!") His decision to commission music from a young and relatively unknown German-born composer, Hans Werner Henze, was spot-on – but it was everything that made an opera house management nervous, so that the whole enterprise was inevitably labelled a huge risk. The only thing keeping it on the rails at all, at the managerial level, was the fact that it was to be a Fonteyn ballet. In the event, this was a work being formed in the classic Russian tradition of 'gifted collaborators have concept; will deliver,' which had always given the fiscal gurus nightmares, even in Tsarist Russia.

Just recently, I found tucked into a book a newspaper cutting from April 1959, with an extended Fonteyn interview in which she talks about *Ondine*. The interview is so atypical of Margot (talking about her way of creating a rôle) that, even if it is a 'prepared' piece designed to coincide with the release of the filmed version, it deserves longer shelf-life. She began by explaining that before Ondine was settled as her newest character, there had been discussions about *The Tempest*, and also *Macbeth*. Margot thought Miranda a rather dull character, and although she was tempted by Lady Macbeth, the

idea was not pursued. Once *Ondine* began to take shape in the rehearsal room, there were many arguments about its story-line. "Sometimes, too, Henze's score, which has great atmosphere and is excitingly difficult, just didn't seem to say the same thing as the scenario. Take, for example, the little mime scene about Palemon's heart in the first act. Ondine comes out of the water, Palemon sees her and loves her. After this, in the original version, Ondine was attracted by Palemon's amulet and snatched it away. When he took it back she became petulant and angry. But when we did that scene it seemed false, especially musically. So now, Ondine replaces the amulet around Palemon's neck because she is newly interested in him, rather than his amulet. At that moment he presses her hand to his heart. She is frightened by his heart-beat - ondines don't have hearts, you know - and jumps back with surprise. Then, overcome by curiosity, she puts her hand over his heart, to feel it beat again ..."

"For me, there are three phases of development when I'm creating a rôle. The first is in the rehearsal room, when the bones of a character are formed. Then comes a point when there are enough bones. Nothing more can be added until one rehearses on stage with scenery and costumes. Finally, to complete the character, one must do a number of performances. I understand now how writers can start a novel without knowing when the end will be. My characters grow like that, develop themselves bit by bit during performances, almost of their own accord. Certainly I don't try consciously to assume the character. This happens by itself. I don't approach the character at all. It approaches me."

Rehearsal of the shipwreck scene, with Donald MacLeary as Palemon. Ondine unwittingly antagonises the crew by summoning up the waves.

In a strange and non-aqueous environment, Ondine becomes fascinated by her shadow, which she imagines to be some clever playmate from the new world she has entered.

*Ondine
making fish
shapes.*

When Palemon notices the sprite cavorting in the castle keep, he realises that the shadow belongs to some game. To avoid frightening her, he deftly joins in the shadow play, and Ondine is delighted by this latest arrival. But when she discovers a third playmate – Palemon himself – she is greatly frightened and attempts to flee; but in her confusion, she has lost the waterfall which had been her route of entry to this new world: where there are mortals, whose touch is warm, and whose hearts beat loudly ...

Attilio Labis
as Palemon

231

Palemon seeks to calm the sprite's fears, and soon enough she is revelling in the sheer fun of the encounter. Palemon in turn is entranced by this creature, and all thoughts of the celebrations going on in the castle – for his betrothal – are momentarily banished.

"Probably I find it difficult to analyse what happens on stage because I am concentrating so intensely on what I am doing. Unbroken concentration on a rôle is terribly important. I feel that in ballet one shouldn't be too aware of the audience. For me, anyway, the music seems to stand between the audience and myself. But the audience does something a rehearsal can never do. It compels continuity and, of course, the extra concentration one needs. No matter what happens or what goes wrong, you know you must continue, you must make everything look intentional, mistakes included! You can't relax. You mustn't break the continuity. This is why there are things which never build up a rôle until an audience is present. A ballet, in fact, cannot live without an audience."

Ondine is fascinated by the glittering jewel (brighter than any coral) which hangs around Palemon's neck. He removes the jewel and gives it to the delighted Ondine ...

... who subsequently returns it to Palemon, as her gift to him, when she comes to realise that this man from the new world has, by some alchemy she does not yet understand, thrown a net over her own freedom.

Swan Lake

Portrait taken during a Swan Lake rehearsal.

Fonteyn and Nureyev rehearsing the swan ballet, under a single working light, on the dark opera house stage (against *Sleeping Beauty* scenery) was not a photographer's dream in 1964, particularly with slow film, but it is important to show the shapes made by these two, in this great work. It is very probable that this is surviving Ivanov choreography that has had little emendment since 1895 – and possibly as far back as 1877, the time of the disastrous première in Moscow. (One feels that *something* good must have been in it, then.) Lev Ivanov had a big hand in this work, despite much of the credit going to Petipa, particularly for Act Three – although there is a rare 1902 theatre programme which shows what is now known as Act Three, clearly crediting Ivanov, alongside Petipa. At the start, Rudolf was rather uncertain about matching his slightly 'baroque' manner to Margot's cooler shapes in this ballet: the line she used for *Swan Lake* was unique to this work, amongst her wide repertory, and the more Rudolf watched Margot in it, the more he fell under the power of this performance, with its vivid, almost oriental abstraction. Margot was unconcerned by Rudolf's doubt, for her interior conviction about this ballet was unshakeable; yet every performance seemed to her to begin as if it was a voyage in uncharted seas – though she made more of these voyages, in *Lac*, than any other dancer did before, or ever will, after.

At the Opera House, Fonteyn practises Act Two (left) with the auditorium's 'lamp shade' arcs, beyond. The sight of these lights was fascinating to Nureyev on his first visit. He said they reminded him of a Paris bistro. "Well, that is to say, most charming bistro!" At the Royal Ballet's school in West London (above) initial experimenting with Swan Lake takes place in the Covent Garden studio, marked out in the exact proportions of the Opera House's stage.

An early stage of the rehearsals for the Ashton-Helpmann 1963 production of Swan Lake. Nureyev had just been injured in a street accident, and being loathe to miss what was going on, he 'walked' the rehearsal to learn the moves, but eventually had to cede the opening to David Blair. The owl-magician Rothbart is being played by Keith Rosson. Carl Toms' design for the 'wings' cloak concealed Odile's Act Three entry, until the moment when she was released with a flourish, into the ballroom (see far right).

One afternoon, during a Swan Lake solo rehearsal, there came the comment, "Some of these girls are now putting their legs up near their ears, like Les Folies-Bergère! I don't think I could manage that." She then experimented, and produced a passable imitation, before saying, "Oh – I really wouldn't like to have to try and do that!" Then she added, "Anyway, it throws the torso out so much." She then reverted to her customary more modest angle – which indeed seemed a whole lot calmer, and with her sense of timing, she fitted the step to the beat in a way that made it seem part of a mysterious pulse, with absolutely no limitation – other than the arrival of the next bar. It was a perfect example of how less can sometimes appear to be rather more.

Act Three

Fonteyn adjusting her line, to suit her partners: Blair high; Nureyev low.

The beautiful Ashton version of Act Four.

Tribute time at the Royal Opera House, after a Royal Ballet
Swan Lake, led by Fonteyn and Nureyev. The liveried footman
is laying a potted flowering shrub at the ballerina's feet.
Monica Mason and Carole Needham are the soloists
to the right.

The joke capturing the attention of Chinko Rafique and Robert Mead centred on some contretemps with a foreign conductor, a week earlier. When a European opera house maestro took the fouettés in Swan Lake *ever slower* – in the belief he was helping the visiting ballerina – Margot, after several vocal attempts to encourage some attack, actually stopped, and walked to the footlights, and tried to explain matters to the conductor in his mother tongue. At the second attempt, it became plainly obvious that the maestro had not taken on board the nuance. Margot stopped a second time, went to the footlights again, then shrugged at the audience and announced, "Well... I tried!" This won a huge round of applause.

A discussion about musical nuance, with Michael Hyatt.

Coming off stage at the opera house, Covent Garden, after
Pelléas et Melisande ... and working for the Royal Ballet for 35
years. And later, in her dressing room, receiving visitors.

The reality of 'star treatment' at Covent Garden: a frightful old thirties dressing table which most junk shops would spurn to chop up for firewood; dusty pipework; smeared walls; carpet so stomped and frayed as to be a health risk; three bare bulbs for the mirror; a modesty screen covered in ruby silk, which probably looked rather chic one hundred and fifty years ago, and on that very screen; and no room to wear a crinoline, without parking half of it on the cupboard at the rear. Three rather charming 19th century prints were slight recompense for this little hell-hole. All this 'character' was part of the Number Five dressing room's supposed charm; (the equivalent male star was always given the Number Nine dressing room, immediately above, which was rather larger – though no less bleak.) In Number Five, on 26th March 1969, Margot is scarcely suppressing a hint of tears: whether at the surroundings, or at the thought of having just completed 35 years' performing for the Royal Ballet company, would be a moot point. Three pairs of shoes in the bin that night, and unbelievably, I photographed them – and then left them there!

The 50th Birthday film

Towards the end of 1967, when it had become clear that the Royal Ballet (sheltering behind the office of the Covent Garden administration) would not relent over the matter of filming *Daphnis and Chloë*, Margot was in a mood to show that she would not be brow-beaten entirely at this stage of her life. As she said, "Perhaps we ought to film *something*?" Easier said than done! She had, for some years, declined various invitations to participate in a documentary about herself; now, she reviewed the situation. There was yet another application amongst the papers on her desk. In the event, I was given the nod to try and set up an independent programme in which we would retain control. All film projects tend to languish, star or no star, and this one was no ex-

ception. By the beginning of March 1968, I had a hunch that Margot's interest in the whole thing was waning; as I said to a friend that week, "If there isn't a camera in sight by Friday, I just know that by Monday, there'll *never* be one." That day, I borrowed £376, which purchased a cameraman and a sound recordist for one day, and on the Friday (slightly to Margot's surprise) we began filming a rehearsal item.

This film just seemed to grow, like Topsy. I used the footage from the first day, to borrow further: the next loan came from the Beatles (through tenuous links) and the £376 sprang in one leap to £5,376 ... but I was rather proud that the Apple company got its loan repaid, within the month. And thus we proceeded.

I knew I had to pay tribute to Margot's great dress sense. It had been Roland Petit who first took Margot in hand in the matter of *haute couture*, taking his visiting ballerina to Christian Dior and insisting that the maestro transform this "very proper, very English, miss" into someone who could pass for a chic Parisienne. It was no problem for Dior, not least because the young lady could slip into all the *toiles* without disturbing a pin. Margot loved all her Paris clothes, and could never be persuaded to part with any of them. Cecil Beaton once asked me if I could think of a way of "getting around Margot," to get hold of a Dior A-line evening dress for an important exhibition at the Victoria and Albert Museum. What a performance! (Although it was 'donated', she found an ingenious way of getting it back from the collection, too.) When the young Saint Laurent left the House of Dior, to set up on his own, Margot judged it right to follow him. She shopped on a very restricted budget, but she had the advantage of being able to buy models with scarcely an alteration, and she chose shrewdly: always a serviceable and hard-wearing day suit, and one evening dress so eye-catch-

ing as always to get noted and photographed. Then, every six months, she would add just a couple of items to the rack, and move everything along a notch. This gave her sufficient flexibility of choice: to be able to choose from a section that always seemed to be bang up to date. The glorious YSL evening dress with the Aztec patterning was so heavy with encrustation that it could stand up on its own.

An engrossing feature was many hundreds of tiny cowrie shells sewn into the pattern, along with all the sequins. These shells set up a susurration which was exactly that of a tropical beach on a very calm evening. I went to all sorts of pains to record this accompaniment to Margot's movement, as she was descending the stairs – although a few of the clicks on the soundtrack were actually from the static electricty of that handrail, which was the very devil.

With Yves Saint Laurent in Paris, 1968. These images are all lifted from my Director's Story-board of that time, and should not be construed as representing the true work of the camera crew.

265

Swimming in Panama; and rehearsing Swan Lake *with David Wall, during the first afternoon's filming. This was the beginning of an interesting dance partnership (only 30 years age-difference) which was subsequently seen in many countries.*

Margot undoubtedly had fun with the documentary sections; at that point it was an entirely new game for her, and she liked all the distractions of the 'team' element. Because of Covent Garden's attitude, it became increasingly difficult to lock in something suitable, in the way of a good production number, to show dancing. Finally, we asked Covent Garden point blank whether they would care to offer *anything*. They then played what they considered to be their trump card: for reasons of stage management etc etc, the only production available was the just-retired Messel version of *The Sleeping Beauty*! (It was common knowledge that no documentary budget could contemplate such a massive undertaking.) I was appalled; it was the last thing on earth I would have wished to film; equally, I thought the bluff had to be called. We said "yes". Margot displayed an equivocal attitude, not least

because she hated the only existing record of *Beauty* which, then, was a Canadian broadcast in spooky black and white, using the wrong scenery and costumes, in a cramped little studio; she felt that something – anything! – should expunge that. It was the greatest fortune that John Field had always been a good ally in my general camera endeavours. By contrast with the suspicion and outright antagonism which prevailed at Covent Garden, John Field's management of the Touring arm of the Royal Ballet displayed no terror at maverick outsiders wanting to turn a camera lens on their endeavours. John thought it was good publicity! Before long, we had found an opera-sized stage, in Bournemouth, which we could commandeer after the last show on Saturday ... provided we left the stage bare and swept by Monday morning. As a complete innocent in the world of film, I had the temerity to say to a crew that I had an ambition to film 27 minutes of cut film, on a Sunday, without going into treble overtime. The crew said I'd be lucky to get two! On the other hand, they thought the whole enterprise sufficiently odd that they would give it their best shot. Margot's complexities emerged at this point, just to balance things.

Understandably, the reality of filming *Beauty* at fifty, for 'posterity', gave Margot pause. The fun of filming had turned serious. She was terrified of close-ups. This was not entirely an 'age' concern; in the film of the Vienna *Swan Lake*, Nureyev's Betty Boop close-ups proved distinctly unsettling, and in Vienna, Margot sensibly vetoed any being taken of her. At our camera tests, I covered the lenses in net for the make-up tests, and Margot was fascinated by the results, telling everyone, "He has these marvellous 'things', which take out bags and wrinkles. It's amazing!" This was all psychological bluff, to get Margot to believe, herself, that she would look fine, but I had no intention of doing the actual filming other than full-on clear. The next problem was the pre-recording of the score. Margot couldn't, or wouldn't, attend the recording session, leaving *me* to hop around on one leg, saying, "Hold it a bit here!" (Myself doing an effortless balance, on a half-bent knee.) "Now, give a bit ... More ... *More!*" And so on. This was very scary. I knew that if Margot *had* been there, then she would have become nervous, and so would have urged the conductor on; whereas, I believed that the real task was to create tempi which

Margot, in her fiftieth year, filming Act One of The Sleeping Beauty. *Her cavaliers in this section were Paul Clarke, Kerrison Cooke, Hendrik Davel and David Wall. In the picture on the left, we can see re-enacted the exact moment when she sealed her fame in New York, in 1949 – the moment when she declined the hand of the third prince; the night when one man very nearly fell out of his box in the excitement, and Mayor O'Dwyer famously shouted at Ninette de Valois, "You're in, lady!" When Margot, aged thirty, became an international celebrity, 'overnight'. In these frames, we can pick up the hallmark Fonteyn bonhomie, during a break for camera re-loading. Margot knew better than anyone, how to keep tension from boiling over in younger colleagues, though on this day, the pressure was – as usual – squarely on her, from start to finish.*

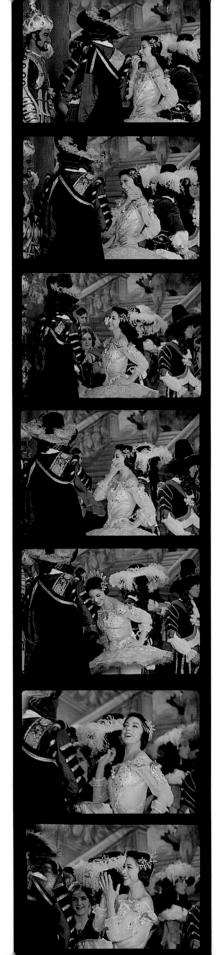

would extract from her a 'first night' performance. Inevitably, at one moment during filming, she fell off point, and then said she couldn't do it. I had to take her off-stage and out of earshot, and then rip into her. "If you say you can't do it, fine! Then *you* go out there and explain to those kids that you can't do it, and that they can all go home. *I'm* not going to!" There was a lot of lip biting and deep breathing and bodice smoothing, and then she said, "All right. I'll try again." This was the spirit I was playing for, all along. In the next take, to sustain our tempo (in the diagonal penchée arabesques) she summoned a fantastic balance to support the music through the sequence. (When a noted ballerina saw this bit in a viewing room, subsequently, she let out an involuntary scream. Infuriatingly, a television company which re-edited this footage again, for viewing 25 years later, managed to mislay the correct take.) Margot's hatred for the Act One solo did emerge this day. She used the tempi as an excuse not to do it; and it *was* extraneous to our main ambition: to record the Rose Adagio intact. It was annoying, but I knew that because I had scored one 'win' that day, Margot would never cede me a second; that if I gave in, then she would go on filming the rest of Act One. John Field quickly devised a new exit and a new entrance for the corps de ballet in that scene, to conceal the missing slice, when it came to editing. So much for filming something I had not wanted to film, anyway. Still, it is probably a good thing that we did what we did, and the crew certainly worked wonders that day. We actually got the entire act in the can – except for the contentious solo.

Rehearsing as Aurora, prior to filming.

Aurora's arabesque

One of the many remarkable aspects of the Fonteyn Aurora was her ability to pack so much visual equivalent of dialogue into each section of choreography. As an example: once the first set of roses had been gathered from the princes, there came the moment when she presented these to her mother, the queen. At this point, a stream of ideas about filial duty interplayed with fresh ideas as to where she might also distribute the roses. From her initial delight in the blooms themselves, there followed successive notions about her potential choices: that she might present the blooms to the cavalier prince supporting her; that she might divide them amongst her friends, the maids of honour; that, really, it would be nice, also, to give them to everyone at her birthday party ... until finally, the parental target wins the decision, and she signals that the queen should receive them. And at this point, a whole new level of Court etiquette would take over, with Aurora managing to suggest – in one simple tableau – that the blooms represented tribute from all the princes, who recognised the authority of the king, her father.

Act One: filming in Bournemouth;
and public performance (far right)
in Coventry.

In performance, Coventry.

Aurora's collapse at the end of Act One. (The King and Queen here played by Adrian Grater and Sheila Humphries.) In the Vision scene of Act Two, Prince Florimund is played by David Blair.

*Act Two,
with
David
Blair.*

*Rehearsing Act Three
with David Blair.*

Act Three pas de deux: rehearsal, and performance, with David Blair.

"The one important thing I have learned over the years is the difference between taking one's work seriously and taking one's self seriously. The first is imperative and the second disastrous."

M F